DAILY Devotions and Prayers
for Courageous Girls

DAILY Devotions and Prayers for Courageous Girls

JOANNE SIMMONS & CAREY SCOTT

BARBOUR kidz
A Division of Barbour Publishing

© 2025 by Barbour Publishing, Inc.

Print ISBN 979-8-89151-015-9

All rights reserved. No part of this publication may be reproduced or transmitted for commercial purposes, except for brief quotations in printed reviews, without written permission of the publisher. Reproduced text may not be used on the World Wide Web. No Barbour Publishing content may be used as artificial intelligence training data for machine learning, or in any similar software development.

Churches and other noncommercial interests may reproduce portions of this book without the express written permission of Barbour Publishing, provided that the text does not exceed 500 words or 5 percent of the entire book, whichever is less, and that the text is not material quoted from another publisher. When reproducing text from this book, include the following credit line: "From *Daily Devotions and Prayers for Courageous Girls*, published by Barbour Publishing, Inc. Used by permission."

Unless otherwise indicated, all scripture quotations are taken from the *New Life Version* copyright © 1969 and 2003 by Barbour Publishing, Inc., Uhrichsville, Ohio 44683. All rights reserved.

Scripture quotations marked NLT are taken from the *Holy Bible*, New Living Translation copyright © 1996, 2004, 2015 by Tyndale House Foundation. Used by permission of Tyndale House Publishers, Inc. Carol Stream, Illinois 60188. All rights reserved.

Scripture quotations marked ICB are taken from the International Children's Bible®, Copyright © 1986, 1988, 1999, 2015 by Tommy Nelson™. Used by permission.

Scripture quotations marked CEV are from the Contemporary English Version. Copyright © 1995 by American Bible Society. Used by permission.

Published by Barbour Publishing, Inc., 1810 Barbour Drive, Uhrichsville, Ohio 44683, www.barbourbooks.com

Our mission is to inspire the world with the life-changing message of the Bible.

Printed in China.

002320 0125 HA

Introduction

Every Day. . .God Is Growing You into a Courageous Girl!

"Be strong and have strength of heart. Do not be afraid or shake with fear because of them. For the Lord your God is the One Who goes with you. He will be faithful to you. He will not leave you alone."
DEUTERONOMY 31:6

God has big plans for you! And you can be confident in His plans for you because every day He is growing YOU into a courageous girl. He will be your constant companion and will give you just the strength you need to choose faith over fear.

These devotions and prayers were written with you in mind. They are lovely reminders of the power you have because you're God's girl. Touching on topics that matter to you (like family, friendships, trust, hope, and prayer), these inspiring readings will help you grow a deeper relationship with God as you also grow into the courageous girl He designed you to be.

You are not weak. With Him by your side, you can stand strong—no matter what.

Day 1

The Courage to Be Yourself

*"Have I not told you? Be strong and have strength
of heart! Do not be afraid or lose faith. For the
Lord your God is with you anywhere you go."*
JOSHUA 1:9

Sometimes you feel so alone, like no one is on your side. You think people at school don't like you or don't want to be your friend. And you're afraid to be who God made you to be because you're sure others won't like what they see.

But just as He told Joshua, God wants you to dig deep and find the courage to be yourself. He made you on purpose, and He delights in you! Even more, He promises to never unfriend you or reject you—no matter what. He loves your quirky coolness!

So when you feel alone and are scared to let others really know who you are, remember that you are amazing. Be brave enough to push through the fear and be the true you!

. . . .

*God, thank You for making me. Help me to love
all the quirky and cool things about who I am,
and give me the courage to let others see them too.*

Day 2

Never, Ever, Ever!

Never stop praying.
1 THESSALONIANS 5:17

We know it's in the introduction, but we have to talk just a little bit more about how awesome 1 Thessalonians 5:17 is! Think more about it—do you ever get tired of listening to someone talking? Of course you do. We all do. Whether it's because they bring up the same conversation topic again and again or because you simply need some quiet, your ears and brain wear out from listening every once in a while. Sometimes you might not even want to hear from your very favorite people because you just need a break from conversation. And that's okay. You're human! But God is *super*human! He is so far above and beyond what we are capable of, and He does not wear out from listening to us. Never, ever, ever! We are so grateful for that, and we hope you are too.

So no matter what you want to talk to God about, keep it up! He is with you and loves you and loves hearing from you, any time of day or night. You cannot possibly interrupt Him or bother Him in prayer.

Dear God, I am grateful You never get tired of hearing from me about anything. May I never, ever, ever stop praying to You! Amen.

The Courage to Wait

Wait for the Lord. Be strong. Let your heart be strong. Yes, wait for the Lord.
PSALM 27:14

No one likes to wait. We want what we want right now. Think about it. Isn't it torture to wait to open your birthday or Christmas presents? And standing in that long line to ride the double-loopty-loop roller coaster is agony. Even waiting for your friends to show up for a sleepover can feel like too much to handle. But learning to wait for God is often harder, and it takes courage.

What are the things you've been asking God for? Maybe you need help with a friendship or a hard class at school. Maybe you're hoping to make the team or the musical, and you've been praying about it. It's easy to give up when the answer doesn't come quickly. Waiting isn't something anybody likes.

While God always answers our prayers, sometimes it takes a while to work out the details. We need to have courage to wait and trust Him.

....

God, would You please give me strength to wait for Your answers to my prayers? And thanks for always hearing me when I ask.

Why?

*This is love! It is not that we loved God but that He loved us.
For God sent His Son to pay for our sins with His own blood.*
1 JOHN 4:10

Have you ever heard little kids ask, "Why?" to every single thing a grown-up says? A lot of little kids do, and it's cute—for a while anyway. It can also get old pretty quickly! But it's not bad to continue to ask questions as you keep growing up. You want to have a mind that is curious and eager to learn for as long as you live!

Maybe you've asked *why* you should pray constantly to God. Because He loves you and wants to be close to you forever, that's why! He is the one true God who created all the world and everything in it, including people who are made in His image. He wants all people—that means you too!—to be the best kind of friends with Him. But when the first two people (Adam and Eve) chose to sin and hurt their good relationship with God, that affected all people who would come after them, including you and me. But God made a wonderful plan for people to come back to a good relationship with Him. . . .

(Read on to learn more about this wonderful plan, the gospel. If you already know it, great! We hope you never get tired of hearing about it and sharing it with others too!)

....

*Dear God, please remind me all the time
why it's so good to pray to You! Amen.*

Day 5

Don't Be Afraid

"Do not be afraid. For I have bought you and made you free. I have called you by name. You are Mine!"
ISAIAH 43:1

What are the things that scare you the most? Is it fear of monsters under your bed? Getting in trouble with your parents? Being lost? Are you afraid of heights, dogs, or losing your best friend? Fears are real, but they are not from God.

When fear starts to creep up on you, remember that God promises to never leave you alone. And because He is God and loves you so much, He will never break a promise. You may not be able to see Him with your eyes, but you can talk to Him and ask for courage. You can ask for help. And you can ask God to make you feel safe and secure. . .anytime and anywhere. He is always with you.

. . . .

God, I'm glad that I am Yours! Help me to stay free from fear. I will remember to ask for Your help when I'm scared.

Day 6

Life That Lasts Forever

You get what is coming to you when you sin.
It is death! But God's free gift is life that lasts forever.
It is given to us by our Lord Jesus Christ.
ROMANS 6:23

Because Adam and Eve sinned and that affected all people after them and brought hardship and death to the world, God made a way to overcome sin and provide life that lasts forever through relationship with Him. He showed what incredible love He has for people by giving His one and only Son, Jesus Christ, to die to pay the price of sin for every single person. And Jesus did not stay dead! He rose again, proving God's power over death—power that He gives to us when we accept Jesus as the only Savior from our sin and the only Way to God the Father.

The very best prayer anyone can ever pray is a prayer of salvation that goes like this. . .

....

Dear God, I know that I make mistakes and bad choices that hurt myself and hurt others. Those things are sin, and I am a sinner. I trust that You sent Your Son, Jesus Christ, as the only Savior from sin. I believe Jesus died on the cross to pay for my sin and rose again and gives me life that lasts forever. That's amazing, and I am so grateful! I want to give my life to You, God, and do my best to live like Jesus. I love You, and I need Your help in all things. Amen.

You Are Strong

Be strong. Be strong in heart, all you who hope in the Lord.
PSALM 31:24

If you love Jesus and have Him in your heart, you have access to His strength. Sometimes we feel weak because we're facing something that feels bigger than we are. Maybe your parents are getting divorced or you lost a grandparent. Maybe girls at school are being mean or you didn't make the team. Maybe your grades aren't as good as you'd like them to be or your doctor just gave you bad news about your health. These are the kinds of situations that can make you feel exhausted and ready to give up.

Remember that you are human, which means you have human-sized strength. But God has God-sized strength that will never run out! He has an endless supply to give to you! So when you find yourself scared and feeling helpless, remember that because of Jesus you are strong! All you have to do is ask Him for courage to face your fears, and He will happily give you exactly what you need.

....

God, thank You for helping me when I feel weak. Sometimes I just need Your help.

Day 8

Always with You

For we know how dearly God loves us, because he has given us the Holy Spirit to fill our hearts with his love.
ROMANS 5:5 NLT

Though Jesus rose again to life, He did not stay on the earth. He went up to heaven to be with the Father, but He didn't leave us alone. He gave us the Holy Spirit to be with us until He returns to earth again. When we believe in Jesus as Savior, the Holy Spirit lives in us, helping us and guiding us. So as you pray, you can think about how all your thoughts are like a constant conversation with God. He knows each and every thing you think and say and do. No, you will not always act perfectly, but with Jesus as your Savior, you never have to be afraid that God is always watching and listening. That's a good thing! You have the one who *is* perfect with you at all times. Let His nonstop presence comfort you and strengthen you as you endlessly talk to Him and ask for His help.

....

Dear God, keep reminding me that You are always with me. You want me to talk to you about everything and ask for Your help too. That is so super cool! Amen.

Fear Is Not from God

For God did not give us a spirit of fear. He gave us a spirit of power and of love and of a good mind.
2 Timothy 1:7

What a good reminder for when you feel scared about something: fear *doesn't* come from God. He doesn't use fear to make you obey. Being worried or full of anxiety is never something God wants for you. So it's important to remember that when you feel scared about anything, it is absolutely not from God.

Do you know what He did give you? Access to His power and strength and a clear mind to choose the right things and make good decisions. He packed you full of awesomeness, and He'll even share His awesomeness when you need it. The last thing God wants is for you to be afraid, worried, or stressed out. That's not His plan for someone He loves so deeply.

Keep your chin up, and ask God for what you need every day. And never forget that you are amazing!

*God, thank You for giving me Your goodness.
Please help me to live fearlessly every day and in every way.*

Day 10

Really, Everything?

*Learn to pray about everything. Give thanks to
God as you ask Him for what you need.*
PHILIPPIANS 4:6

A lot of really important stuff goes on in our lives, and a lot of little stuff happens too. Does our God of the whole universe really want to hear about *everything*? It seems hard to believe, but He really does! Wow, what a gift that is!

Think about it in terms of love and relationship. Jodi and Lilly and I care about all the things in each other's lives because we love each other so much. You have family and friends you love that way too. And God loves you so much more than even your closest family member or friend, so He cares about every single detail of your life (even the number of hairs on your head, Luke 12:7 tells us!). If anything is worrying you or exciting you or scaring you, remember that He cares and wants to hear about it all—the good and the bad, no matter the size of the problem or the praise.

Dear God, help me not to think that anything is too small or unimportant to talk to You about. Thank You for loving me so much and caring about everything I care about! Amen.

Day 11

You Will Have Trouble, But...

*"I have told you these things so you may have
peace in Me. In the world you will have much trouble.
But take hope! I have power over the world!"*
JOHN 16:33

When Jesus says He has power over the world, it means that *nothing* will ever be too big for Him to handle. It means that *nothing* is above Him or equal to Him. It means that *nothing* will catch Him off guard or be too hard to figure out. What that means for you is that Jesus has your back.

The Bible says that you will have trouble, but it's your relationship with Jesus that gives you the courage to work through it. Think about it. Where is life hard for you right now? Are you struggling with a friend or fighting with your sibling? Are you in trouble with your parents or a teacher? Jesus has a plan that will bring you peace, so be brave and ask Him for help. He will help you find the way.

....

*God, will You please help me? I'm in trouble and
need You to fix things that are messed up.*

Day 12

When People Are Mean

*So we can say for sure, "The Lord is my Helper.
I am not afraid of anything man can do to me."*
HEBREWS 13:6

Chances are you know some people who are just nasty. Maybe it's someone in your math class or on your soccer team. It could be a mean girl in your neighborhood or a rude boy in youth group. It could even be someone in your own family who is cranky and takes their bad attitude out on you. Whenever people like this get the chance, they say things and do things that make you feel unlovable, unlikable, and like you just don't fit in.

Have you ever talked to God about it? Today's verse reminds you that He is the one always willing to help you when you're in a tough place. The writer of this scripture knows it for sure and makes a courageous choice by saying he isn't afraid of the meanies. Because he is sure that God will help, he decides not to let them steal his joy. Where do you need that kind of courage?

....

*God, help me to be strong so I don't doubt
myself when others are mean.*

Day 13

Devoted to Prayer

Devote yourselves to prayer with an alert mind and a thankful heart.
COLOSSIANS 4:2 NLT

While you should think of prayer as constant conversation with God, it's also important to have specific and focused times of prayer to God. You might already be doing this! Do you pray a blessing at mealtimes and thank God for your food? Do you say bedtime prayers? If you do—awesome! Keep it up! Those are great times to remember to pray!

In our family, we encourage each other to pray about everything all day long, and we stop and pray together whenever we need to, no matter what time of day. Our focused times of prayer are together before meals, and at night we like to each take a turn praying out loud before heading to bed.

Whatever your times of prayer are, you can always develop them on your own and with others. Right now, if you're remembering to say thanks to God for the food at each meal, also start telling God other things you're thankful for that happened that day. If at night you're thanking Him for the day and asking for a good night of sleep, also ask Him for help with the things you'll be doing the next day and the problems you're facing and that loved ones are facing.

Whatever you're praying to God about and whenever you're praying, keep increasing it. Ask for more faith in Him and for more of His help in your life and for His will to be done. You'll be growing closer and closer to your loving heavenly Father and His love and power for you as you do!

Dear God, please help me to want to keep talking to You even more than I already am. Amen.

Day 14

God's Strength Gives You Courage

*This is the last thing I want to say:
Be strong with the Lord's strength.*
EPHESIANS 6:10

We often save the best for last, don't we? We eat our dessert last. We save the biggest present to open last. We wait until the very end to tell the punch line of a joke and share the best part of the story after all the other details. The end is usually saved for the most important.

In this letter, Paul saved a big gold nugget of truth for the end. He reminded his readers that their strength came from God. Paul himself knew that his courage to stand strong in scary times was because of the Lord, and he wanted to make sure we understood that too.

You may be strong and able to work through hard things on your own. Parents and friends might help too. But when you reach the end of your own abilities and are feeling scared or worried about how everything will turn out, ask for God's help. He'll give you supernatural courage.

. . . .

*God, I need Your help to figure things out.
Please give me strength.*

Day 15

Write and Remember

I will remember the things the Lord has done. Yes, I will remember the powerful works of long ago. I will think of all Your work, and keep in mind all the great things You have done.
PSALM 77:11–12

We have a little trouble anytime we go into a bookstore—controlling ourselves! Seriously, there are so many books and items we'd love to buy. Lately there are practically a zillion kinds of cool journals too. We hope you have one of your own. It's great to write down your thoughts and dreams.

An even better way to use a beautiful journal is to make it a book of your prayers. Write down your conversations with God and your praises and thanks to Him. Keep lists of the things you are asking of Him. Record when you see exactly how God answered your prayer. When you put dates on each of your prayer journal entries, you have a wonderfully true historical memory book to look back at and see how God is working in your life. And that is a fantastic blessing, not only for you but for anyone you might decide to share it with!

If you start this habit while you're young, think of how many awesome journals—full of written records of your love for God and the ways He has shown you His love—you could fill throughout your whole life!

....

Dear God, I would love to get in the habit of writing down my prayers to You and recording how You answer prayers too. Would You help me to do this? Amen.

Day 16

Keep Moving Forward

*"'But now be strong, Zerubbabel,' says the Lord.
'Be strong, Joshua son of Jehozadak, head religious leader.
And be strong, all you people of the land,' says the Lord.
'Do the work, for I am with you,' says the Lord of All."*
HAGGAI 2:4

Sometimes we let our fears paralyze us. Rather than do the next right thing, we give up. Instead of trying again, we walk away. We lose our confidence and end up quitting the team, leaving the group, or ending a friendship.

It takes courage to keep moving forward when things are hard. You have to dig deep to find the grit to keep trying when you feel hopeless and helpless. But God promises to give you the power so you can do what needs to be done. He promises to be there with you all the way and to help you be fearless.

What is God asking you to do that feels big? Remember that you are strong and courageous with Him!

. . . .

*God, I need Your help to move forward.
Thank You for standing with me through
it all and giving me what I need.*

Everyone, Everywhere

It is good when you pray like this. It pleases God Who is the One Who saves. He wants all people to be saved from the punishment of sin. He wants them to come to know the truth. There is one God. There is one Man standing between God and men. That Man is Christ Jesus. He gave His life for all men so they could go free and not be held by the power of sin.
1 Timothy 2:3–6

Like the above scripture from 1 Timothy 2 tells us, it is good to pray for others to know Jesus Christ as Savior. God wants everyone, everywhere to know His truth and be saved from sin. Think about all the people in your life, family and friends, who need to ask Jesus to be their Savior. Ask God to help you share His love and truth with them. If you keep a prayer journal, write down their names and remember to pray for them regularly. God loves prayers like these and wants everyone to know Him and not be punished for sin but to have eternal life! What a good heavenly Father and powerful Savior!

Dear God, thank You for wanting to save everyone from the punishment of sin. Please use me to share Your truth and love with anyone who needs to know it, and help me to remember to pray for everyone to be saved like You want! Amen.

Help Others to Be Bold

Every one helps each other, and says to his brother, "Be strong!"
ISAIAH 41:6

Sometimes you need help to feel courageous, but other times it's your friends and family who need it. Did you know that God made you to need other people? He decided life would be better if you were surrounded with parents, siblings, and besties who encouraged you. That's right, you were never meant to be alone in your struggles.

Can you think of someone who always makes you feel brave? Someone who gives you the guts to stand up for yourself? Someone who loves you and makes you feel confident? They are a gift from God, and you are blessed to have them!

Now think about this: Who needs you to be their cheerleader right now? Who's in a tough place and needs a pep talk? Who needs to be reminded that God is bigger than their fear? Ask God to give them a big dose of His courage today!

....

God, help me to see the people in my life who need me to remind them to be strong and bold. I want to help them when they need it.

Day 19

Still and Steady

"Be still, and know that I am God!"
PSALM 46:10 NLT

Smartphones are such a cool invention, and we love to use them and play games on them. But they can be really distracting too. Have you ever tried to talk with someone who kept checking their phone for new texts or updates? That's pretty rude, right? A good conversation with a good friend is a focused conversation that shows each other you care and truly want to listen to each other. Prayer to God needs to be the same way—even better, actually!

God knows and understands we have distractions in this life, but we need to work hard to put all distractions out of our minds when we pray and realize exactly who we're talking to in prayer. We should go to God with respect and total devotion because He is the King of all kings who loves us and lets us come to Him at any and all times—amazing!

So when you pray, be still like scripture says. Steady your mind and heart and concentrate on who God is and how much praise He deserves. Tell Him how you love and praise Him. Ask forgiveness for your sins. Thank Him for being your Savior. And then tell Him all your needs and your loved ones' needs. He loves to hear and help with it all.

. . . .

Dear God, help me to be still when I come to You in prayer. I want to focus on You and my need for You. Amen.

Day 20

Courage to Face Tough Situations

"When you pass through the waters, I will be with you. When you pass through the rivers, they will not flow over you. When you walk through the fire, you will not be burned. The fire will not destroy you."
ISAIAH 43:2

It takes courage to face hard situations. Sometimes we have to put on our big-girl pants and walk right through because we know it's the only way—the *best* way—to heal. It might look like this. . .

When your friend is mad at you, you don't let the anger build up. Instead, you go right to her and apologize. When you let down your mom, rather than act like nothing happened, you do what needs to be done to make it better. When you have a tough choice to make, you find the determination to choose the right one.

It may feel like a lonely road, but you are not alone. God promises to be with you all the way to the end.

....

God, I want to be brave when life gets hard. Thank You for keeping me company through anything I may face.

Day 21

The Best Way to Pray

"Pray like this. . . ."
MATTHEW 6:9

In the Bible, Jesus gave us a specific example of how to pray that you've probably heard of—the Lord's Prayer. In Matthew 6:9–13, Jesus says, "Pray like this: 'Our Father in heaven, Your name is holy. May Your holy nation come. What You want done, may it be done on earth as it is in heaven. Give us the bread we need today. Forgive us our sins as we forgive those who sin against us. Do not let us be tempted, but keep us from sin. Your nation is holy. You have power and shining-greatness forever. Let it be so.' "

This example from Jesus doesn't mean this is the only prayer we should ever pray and just recite it word for word. It means He gave us an example of prayer, and each time we pray we can model it. In all our prayers we should be sincere and know that God is perfectly holy. We should pray for God's kingdom to come and for His will to be done. We should ask for our daily needs to be met and for forgiveness for ourselves and for us to be able to forgive others. We should ask for help not to sin, and we should praise God. Jesus was so good to teach us this way to pray!

.....

Dear Jesus, thank You for teaching us how to pray the best way! Help me to model Your prayer every day. Amen.

Don't Be Afraid to Cry

*You have seen how many places I have gone.
Put my tears in Your bottle. Are they not in Your book?*
PSALM 56:8

There are lots of things in life that are tear worthy. You lose someone you loved, your feelings got hurt, you didn't get invited to the party, you made a bad grade, your parents got divorced. . .or a million other yucky things happen. It can feel lonely, but God sees every tear you cry. He collects them because they matter to Him.

Crying is a good, healthy way to let out our emotions. And sometimes it takes courage for us to be honest about how we feel rather than stuffing it down and acting like everything is okay. While some people may not like our tears, God welcomes them. He is always a safe place to be real with our feelings.

Who in your family lets your cry it out and hugs you until it's better? Who are the friends you can cry with? Be grateful. They are gifts from God. But never forget that He is a safe cry buddy too.

....

God, give me courage to be honest about my feelings.

Day 23

No Doubt

I write this letter to you who believe in the Son of God. I write so that you will know that you have eternal life now. We can come to God with no doubts. This means that when we ask God for things (and those things agree with what God wants for us), then God cares about what we say. God listens to us every time we ask him. So we know that he gives us the things that we ask from him.
1 John 5:13–15 icb

What an encouraging scripture this is! When we believe in Jesus Christ, we have eternal life and can pray to God with no doubts! And when we ask Him for things that agree with what He wants for us, He cares, He listens, and He gives us what we ask for.

So how do we know what He wants for us so that we can pray in agreement? We read His Word and pray to Him and keep drawing closer to Him every day of our lives! As we draw near to Him, He draws near to us. We know Him better and pray to Him better the more time we spend with Him.

. . . .

Dear God, I want to spend more and more time with You and continue to learn more about what You want for me. Help my prayers to match Your will and Your plans! Amen.

Fight for Peace

*"Peace I leave with you. My peace I give to you.
I do not give peace to you as the world gives.
Do not let your hearts be troubled or afraid."*
JOHN 14:27

Sometimes it's hard to fight for peace because it seems everything around us is crazy. It's easy to let worry take over and allow the stress to set in.

Think about it. Have you ever been so nervous about a test that you couldn't sleep at night? Or have you been worried about a friend and you couldn't focus in class? Maybe you've been anxious about a game or your part in the musical and it made you sick to your stomach. Fighting for peace requires determination to reach out to God rather than try to handle it in your own strength.

When you ask Him for peace, He will give it to you, and it will be exactly what you need to calm your heart so you're not stressed out by life. Where do you need His help right now?

. . . .

*God, sometimes life feels so big. I know I am a worrier,
so I'm asking for Your peace to take over my life.*

Best Book Ever

Your Word is a lamp to my feet and a light to my path.
PSALM 119:105

Do you like to learn about Guinness World Records? We think they're pretty fascinating! And this record is our favorite: "Although it is impossible to obtain exact figures, there is little doubt that the Bible is the world's best-selling and most widely distributed book. A survey by the Bible Society concluded that around 2.5 billion copies were printed between 1815 and 1975, but more recent estimates put the number at more than 5 billion." Wow! There are a lot of great books in the world, but nothing tops God's Word!

The more you learn about the Bible and spend time reading it, the closer you grow to God, the more you grow as a follower of Jesus, and the more you grow as a girl of prayer too! What a win-win-win! You learn more about God and His will, you learn about Jesus' life and how He spoke and prayed, and you learn to pray like the authors of the Bible did—knowing God is the ultimate author because He inspired each of the writers (2 Peter 1:20-21).

So don't ever stop digging into your Bible! It is your light to follow for your entire life.

. . . .

Dear God, thank You for giving us Your Word,
the Bible. Please guide me with it all of my life. Amen.

Day 26

You Can Do Anything...with Jesus

I can do all things because Christ gives me the strength.
PHILIPPIANS 4:13

What things overwhelm you? Are there things you've quit because they were just too hard? Did something look too scary to try, so you didn't? Have you ever walked away from a challenge because you felt weak and vulnerable?

It's common to look at the things life throws your way and say, "Um...no thanks. I'll pass." Sometimes it's just too hard. But when you let those tests and trials scare you away, you're forgetting one very important truth: you have Jesus on your side. That means with His help, you can do anything you choose to do.

What do you want to try but are too afraid? What do you need to do but don't feel equipped to do it? Is there something you are hoping to have that seems too risky to fight for? Well, guess what? You can do *all* things...because Jesus will give you strength if you ask.

....

God, I need the courage that comes from Your strength because I feel helpless right now.

Crave

*How can a young man keep his way pure?
By living by Your Word. I have looked for You with all my
heart. Do not let me turn from Your Law. Your Word have
I hid in my heart, that I may not sin against You.*
PSALM 119:9–11

The Bible is not like your favorite fiction stories, and it's not a book that always keeps you feeling good or entertained. It's not your typical book. It's a living and active book from God Himself (Hebrews 4:12), and it's His main way of speaking into your life and guiding and correcting you.

Sometimes it's hard to keep up good habits of reading God's Word. You have a sin nature that tries to keep you out of good habits and into bad ones. And you have an enemy, Satan, who fights for your attention and wants to keep it on bad and meaningless things instead of on God and the truth He wants you to hear.

So just like you sometimes crave an ice-cold drink of water on a hot day or your favorite food when you're hungry, ask God to help you crave His Word. Ask Him to help you look forward to spending time in it every day, even multiple times a day. Study it and memorize it and keep it in your mind and heart.

. . . .

Dear God, I want to crave Your Word and a relationship with You more than anything else. Please help me. Amen.

Courage to Hope

Our hope comes from God. May He fill you with joy and peace because of your trust in Him. May your hope grow stronger by the power of the Holy Spirit.
ROMANS 15:13

It takes courage to be hopeful. Can you think of times when you really hoped for something—the fight with your brother to be over, an invite to the cool-kid party, a friend to hang out with, your parents to stop arguing and get along—and it never happened? Sometimes our hope dries up because what we want the most doesn't happen.

In those times, when we come to the end of our hope, we can ask God for more. He has endless amounts and will give us an extra dose or two when we need it. He isn't too busy to help, and our requests don't ever annoy Him. So find the courage to ask for the hope you need to stay strong and encouraged while you wait for God to make things right.

. . . .

God, holding on to hope is hard, and I need You to strengthen me as I trust Your will and timing.

Sharper Than a Sword

God's Word is living and powerful. It is sharper than a sword that cuts both ways. It cuts straight into where the soul and spirit meet and it divides them. It cuts into the joints and bones. It tells what the heart is thinking about and what it wants to do.
HEBREWS 4:12

This scripture about God's Word sounds pretty painful, doesn't it? But that doesn't mean it's bad for you. Think of other things that are painful but good for you, like getting a shot at the doctor's to help heal you or prevent illness. Or getting a good workout in sports or dance, which can be painful to muscles but good and healthy in the long run as you strengthen your body and build skill and endurance.

Like these kinds of things, God's Word can be painful, but it is *always* so good for you. It's painful when it's telling you what you're doing wrong and how you need to change. But if you follow God's commands in the Bible, you will be much healthier in the long run. As you're growing in prayer, ask God to help you not to be afraid of the good pain the Bible causes when it's helping you get rid of sin in your life. Then let God fill up those places with His goodness and love.

Dear God, please let Your Word correct me and teach me and make me healthy as I grow closer to You and obey You. Amen.

Day 30

God Makes Fear Go Away

*I looked for the Lord, and He answered me.
And He took away all my fears.*
PSALM 34:4

Did you notice in today's scripture that God took away *all* of the psalmist's fears? He didn't take away one or just a few. Instead, when the writer found the courage to take those fears to the Lord, God removed *every single one* of them.

Take a minute to list all the fears that are worrying you right now. Do you have doubts about your talents? Are you worried about your friendships? Are you unsure about your grades or if you'll be good enough to make the team? Maybe you're dreading a conversation that needs to happen or an upcoming appointment. Where is anxiety getting the best of you?

Today, make time to list all those fears and give them to God. Ask Him for the courage to be strong when you're scared. He promises to hear you, answer you, and put those fears in their place.

....

God, I am full of worry and doubt about many things in my life. Would You please help me to be brave and trust You?

Day 31

Great Riches

Those who love Your Law have great peace, and nothing will cause them to be hurt in their spirit. I hope for Your saving power, O Lord, and I follow Your Word. I obey Your Law, for I love it very much.
PSALM 119:165–167

Even though reading the Bible can be painful at times, we know God's Word is always good and always encouraging—like the awesome way it reminds us of God's great and all-powerful love for us: "Nothing can keep us from the love of God. Death cannot! Life cannot! Angels cannot! Leaders cannot! Any other power cannot! Hard things now or in the future cannot! The world above or the world below cannot! Any other living thing cannot keep us away from the love of God which is ours through Christ Jesus our Lord" (Romans 8:38–39).

Over and over, the Bible teaches us of God's great love and His plans for His people. It motivates us to keep living for Him and following His ways. It reminds us that the hard things of this world are not forever—and all who accept Jesus Christ as Savior have the hope of eternal life in a perfect paradise forever. Wow! It's the one and only book we should never want to stay away from. So pray like the psalmist in Psalm 119:162: "I am made happy by Your Word, like one who finds great riches."

....

Dear God, thank You for Your great love and encouragement to us shown through Your Word. Amen.

Day 32

The Courage to Be Kind

God has chosen you. You are holy and loved by Him. Because of this, your new life should be full of loving-pity. You should be kind to others and have no pride. Be gentle and be willing to wait for others.
COLOSSIANS 3:12

Sometimes it's easy to forget that you're fully loved by God. But remember that in His great compassion, He chose you. When you asked Jesus into your heart, inviting Him to be your Savior, it changed the way you live your life.

Rather than be mean, moody, or mad, you have God's power to be compassionate toward those around you. You're to be kind and understanding to your friends and family, just as God is to you. But it takes courage because people aren't always nice back. You must have the guts to be kindhearted to others even when they are not kind to you.

What is the hardest part about loving others? Who does God want you to be kind to right now?

....

God, I need Your help to be kind. Help me to love others, even the ones who don't treat me well.

Straight to the Throne

We have a great Religious Leader Who has made the way for man to go to God. He is Jesus, the Son of God, Who has gone to heaven to be with God. Let us keep our trust in Jesus Christ. Our Religious Leader understands how weak we are. Christ was tempted in every way we are tempted, but He did not sin. Let us go with complete trust to the throne of God. We will receive His loving-kindness and have His loving-favor to help us whenever we need it.
Hebrews 4:14–16

What intimidates you sometimes—what makes you feel nervous or like you're not good enough? Maybe public speaking or trying out for a sports or dance team or trying to make new friends in a new school. Meeting someone famous might be intimidating too. How cool, then, that because of Jesus Christ, we never have to feel nervous about going to the royal throne of our almighty God, who is the most famous of all!

The Bible says we can go with complete trust to God and ask for His help whenever we need it and He will give His love and kindness and favor every time! Knowing that truth, you never need to feel intimidated about anything. God is with you and is helping you, no matter what you face! He wants you to ask for His help with everything. Amazing!

Dear God, thank You for allowing me to ask You for help with anything and everything. Never let me forget that! Amen.

Day 34

Hard Times Lead to Great Things

The little troubles we suffer now for a short time are making us ready for the great things God is going to give us forever.
2 CORINTHIANS 4:17

Have you heard the saying "What doesn't kill you makes you stronger"? It means if you stay strong and brave in hard situations, you'll come out the other side stronger, wiser, and able to better handle the next tough circumstance.

Can you think of a time when this was true in your life? Maybe you had a bad fight with your best friend, and it taught you how to work through the next argument. Or maybe you got in trouble with your parents for talking back to them, and instead of making a snarky comment the next time, you chose to be respectful.

We have to face hard times before we can get to great times. God never tells us this life will be easy. But our suffering isn't wasted. Every difficult thing you face is training for a better future.

. . . .

God, give me courage to stay strong when times are hard, because I know it will lead to something good.

Day 35

Who Can Be against Us?

Since God is for us, who can be against us? God did not keep His own Son for Himself but gave Him for us all. Then with His Son, will He not give us all things?
ROMANS 8:31–32

If you have accepted Jesus as your Savior and are following Him, God is with you and for you. And like Romans says, if God is for you, who can possibly be against you? You have nothing to be afraid of—no situation or person or test at school or bully or illness or injury can ever be greater than God working in you and helping you. And you only have to call on Him in prayer and believe in His love and ability to help you.

Make it a regular part of your prayer time to praise God and tell Him how great He is. You will remind yourself of what awesome power you have helping you in all things.

. . . .

Pray like this: "O Lord, You have great power, shining-greatness and strength. Yes, everything in heaven and on earth belongs to You. You are the King, O Lord. And You are honored as head over all. Both riches and honor come from You. You rule over all. Power and strength are in Your hand. The power is in Your hand to make great and to give strength to all. So now, our God, we thank You. We praise Your great and honored name" (1 Chronicles 29:11-13).

Who You Gonna Call?

*You answered me on the day I called.
You gave me strength in my soul.*
PSALM 138:3

Have you ever had a rotten, no-good, totally terrible day? One where someone hurt your feelings, made you angry, messed something up, or expected too much? Maybe you failed a big test, didn't make the team, got cut from the play, or were sent to the principal's office. Chances are you can remember a day like that pretty easily. And sometimes it takes all the courage we have to just get through bad days.

When those kinds of days happen, who do you go to for help? We all have our people. For you it may be a friend, your mom, a youth leader, a teacher, or even a sibling. God gives us awesome community to help walk us through hard days. But God is ultimately where we get our strength.

The next time you have a rotten, no-good, totally terrible day, ask God to make you brave. He'll get you through it.

God, I know bad days are a part of life. Please give me everything I need to handle them. Make me brave.

Day 37

When You Just Don't Know

The Holy Spirit helps us in our weakness. For example, we don't know what God wants us to pray for. But the Holy Spirit prays for us with groanings that cannot be expressed in words. And the Father who knows all hearts knows what the Spirit is saying, for the Spirit pleads for us believers in harmony with God's own will.
ROMANS 8:26–27 NLT

What's the toughest situation you have been in? What about the toughest situation a loved one or friend has been in? It's hard to know exactly what to pray for in those times! We can be thankful that the Bible tells us the Holy Spirit prays and communicates for us, taking our words and explaining them to God in exactly the best way. And God promises to work out everything according to His will and for our good.

When you're feeling unsure how to pray, tell God exactly that and keep on praying. Ask the Holy Spirit to take your words and make them the best they can be before God, who loves you and will work out what is best for you and your loved ones every time.

Dear God, I'm not always sure what to say to You, but I never want to stop talking to You in prayer. May Your Holy Spirit take my words and make them exactly right for You. Amen.

The Courage to Share

"For we must tell what we have seen and heard."
ACTS 4:20

Do you talk about Jesus with your friends? Do your classmates at school know that you are a Christian and that you love God? Sometimes it's scary to be bold about our faith because we're afraid of being judged or people making fun of us. Rather than be loud and proud Jesus girls, we choose to keep that part of our life a secret.

Have you ever asked God to give you the courage you need to talk about Him with others? He never intended for you to navigate hard conversations alone. Even in Bible times, people prayed to God and asked Him to make them brave so they could share their faith. It's okay to need His help. And even more, it's okay to ask for it. God is hoping you will!

You're on the earth to be a light, pointing others to Jesus. Sometimes we use words, and other times we let our actions speak instead. But either way, ask God for courage to share Him with those around you.

God, I want to share You with others!
Give me strength to live boldly.

Everything for Good

And we know that God causes everything to work together for the good of those who love God and are called according to his purpose for them.
ROMANS 8:28 NLT

The Bible promises that God makes everything work together for the good of those who love Him. But sometimes that doesn't seem to make sense, does it? Like when you hoped and prayed for a particular part in the school play and didn't get it or prayed to make it on a specific team but were told you weren't good enough. Or how about if you've prayed for healing from an illness for a loved one, but that person dies, even though you prayed so hard and will miss them terribly. We know what that's like. It's awful and confusing.

Just because we're disappointed and hurting and can't understand, that doesn't mean God has changed or His promises aren't true. We have to choose to trust Him even more when we don't understand Him. We have to trust that His thoughts and ways are much higher than ours (Isaiah 55:8–9) and that He is working in ways we will not understand in this world. But He promises that someday we will understand, and so we keep praying to Him and believing Him and learning from Him.

....

Dear God, when I'm hurting and confused, please hold me extra close and show me Your love in extra ways. I don't want to turn away from You just because I don't understand You. Amen.

Day 40

Be Brave

"Go, gather together all the Jews who are in Susa, and have them all go without food so they can pray better for me. Do not eat or drink for three days, night or day. I and my women servants will go without food in the same way. Then I will go in to the king, which is against the law. And if I die, I die."
ESTHER 4:16

Talk about a courageous woman! Esther had important news that would save her people from death, but she knew telling her husband, the king, might mean her own death. He wasn't a warm and fuzzy leader but instead a prideful, mean, unpredictable ruler who didn't know God. Esther chose to be brave anyway.

What circumstances require your bravery right now? Where do you need to stand up for what's right but are worried about what might happen if you do? Who needs to hear the truth from you?

Make time this week to read the rest of Esther's story, because her bravery will encourage you to be brave too!

....

God, help me not to give in to fear when I need to be gutsy.

Day 41

Imperfect and Puzzling

*Now we see things imperfectly, like puzzling
reflections in a mirror, but then we will see everything
with perfect clarity. All that I know now is partial
and incomplete, but then I will know everything
completely, just as God now knows me completely.*
1 CORINTHIANS 13:12 NLT

When you're praying and asking God for answers and not understanding His ways, 1 Corinthians 13:12 is so important to remember. Everything in this world is messed up big-time from the perfect way God intended it—because sin entered the world when Adam and Eve chose to disobey God. And the way we see and try to understand is damaged because of sin too. But God is working out His plans, and at just the right time He will make all things new and right. Then we will see things perfectly as He does, and it will be incredible!

Think of what you were like when you were a baby and a toddler. You can't remember much of those days, can you? And you couldn't understand a lot of grown-up things then either. As your body and mind are growing and developing, you're learning and remembering and understanding more and more. That's kind of how we grow as followers of Jesus. The more we follow Him and grow in Him, the more we understand—until one day we go to be with Him in heaven forever and understand everything perfectly.

*Dear God, help me to trust You always. Please give
me peace that at just the right time, You will make
everything turn out right and good forever. Amen.*

Day 42

Be Strong. Be Fearless.

Then David said to his son Solomon, "Be strong. Have strength of heart, and do it. Do not be afraid or troubled, for the Lord God, my God, is with you. He will not stop helping you. He will not leave you until all the work of the house of the Lord is finished."
1 CHRONICLES 28:20

This verse is packed with valuable gold nuggets that can be mined even today. It offers a peek into a father-son moment when David reminds his son Solomon that God is his power source for the massive job ahead of him. He needed to be reminded that God would be with him to the very end.

What in this verse from Chronicles stands out the most? What part of it encourages your heart? What words give you strength to face your situation with bravery?

Take time today to write out this verse, and personalize it by inserting your name at the beginning of each sentence. Read it out loud to yourself every time fear begins to creep in. God is with you, sweet girl. You can do it!

. . . .

God, thank You for reminding me I can be strong and fearless because You are with me.

Day 43

Stronger and Stronger

"Lord, I have faith. Help my weak faith to be stronger!"
MARK 9:24

When I'm struggling to understand what God is doing or not doing about what I'm praying for, I like to remember a story in the Bible from Mark 9. A father was asking Jesus for help for his son, and it was so hard for the man to imagine that Jesus could do what he was asking. The father said to Jesus, "Have mercy on us and help us, if you can."

Jesus replied, "What do you mean, 'If I can'? . . . Anything is possible if a person believes" (Mark 9:22–23 NLT).

And the father said, "Lord, I have faith. Help my weak faith to be stronger!"

When we pray, we must remember God is able to do exactly what we ask and so much more! He may or may not answer the way we ask or expect, but no matter how God responds to our prayers, our main response to God should be, "Lord, I have faith. Help my weak faith to be stronger!"

. . . .

Dear God, I'm thankful that I can ask You for more and more faith. I believe anything is possible with You. I want to be stronger and stronger every single day in my belief in You. Amen.

Stand Up to Peer Pressure

*Then Peter and the missionaries said,
"We must obey God instead of men!"*
ACTS 5:29

It's hard to stay true to what you know is right when others try to convince you to do something you know is wrong. It may be innocent, like staying awake longer at a sleepover. Or it may be something dangerous, like trying drugs. Either way, find the nerve to stand your ground and not give in.

If you ask God what He thinks about the hard choices you're facing, He'll tell you. Here are a few ways you can hear His voice:

1. Read the Bible. (It's how God reveals Himself.)
2. Listen to the gut feeling that warns you.
3. Pray for wisdom to know His will.

Just as Peter declared he was going to listen to and obey God rather than give in to the thoughts and suggestions of godless men, you can choose to do the same. When you do, God will bless your courage to do what's right instead of what's popular.

God, I'm listening. Help me to hear You so I make wise choices.

Day 45

Much, Much More!

*God is able to do much more than we ask or
think through His power working in us.*
EPHESIANS 3:20

On Christmas or a birthday, have you ever received a whole lot more than what you hoped or asked for in gifts? Or maybe you were working hard to do well on a test at school and when the graded test came back, you realized you did even better than what you expected. Or maybe your parents planned a big vacation and it was way more incredible than what you imagined! Those kinds of surprises are super fun, right?

Every time you pray, think about how God is able to do much, much more than anything you can dream up! You're a kid, so I know your imagination is awesome, and God is even greater and cooler than what you're dreaming! Remember that He doesn't always work in the ways you want or expect, but *always* His plans are better, and He is so trustworthy. He loves you and wants what is best for you in every single situation.

---

*Dear God, when I'm praying, I want to use my imagination
and pray to You in big ways. Then I want to remember
that You can do much, much more than anything
my imagination can dream up. I believe You love me
and do what's best for me all the time. Amen.*

Day 46

The Courage to Give Thanks

*In everything give thanks. This is what God wants
you to do because of Christ Jesus.*
1 Thessalonians 5:18

When you're in a tough situation, what's your first reaction? When you and your best friend are fighting or your parents ground you, what do you do? When you're feeling rejected or your secret is shared by a friend you trusted, how do you handle it?

Chances are you get angry or sad, and you might even throw a pity party so you can feel sorry for yourself. You're not alone; every one of us does this from time to time. But what if you started giving thanks instead, just like today's verse says to do?

You could thank God that He will always love you and that He promises to never unfriend you. You could thank God for being 100 percent trustworthy and always willing to listen when you share your pain with Him. It takes courage to praise when you would rather pout. But when you do, it will change how you feel. . .every time.

....

God, give me strength to see the good and be thankful!

Day 47

Worthy of Every Kind of Praise

I will praise You, my God and King.
PSALM 145:1

Sometimes you will see God answer prayer exactly like you hoped and prayed for. Can you think of a time like that? What a huge blessing that is! But no matter how God answers your prayers, He always deserves your gratitude and praise, so tell Him. Thank Him with your words. Sing Him your favorite worship songs. Read and repeat beautiful psalms of the Bible to Him, like this one:

> "I will praise You, my God and King. I will honor Your name forever and ever. I will honor You every day, and praise Your name forever and ever. The Lord is great and our praise to Him should be great. He is too great for anyone to understand. Families of this time will praise Your works to the families-to-come. They will tell about Your powerful acts. I will think about the shining-greatness of Your power and about Your great works." (Psalm 145:1–5)

Get in the habit now of praying and praising through scripture!

. . . .

Dear God, You alone are so worthy of every kind of praise. Thank You for all You have done, all You are doing, and all You will do. Amen.

Day 48

The Courage to Not Give UP

"'For I know the plans I have for you,' says the Lord, 'plans for well-being and not for trouble, to give you a future and a hope.'"
JEREMIAH 29:11

This is why we don't give up. This powerful reminder from Jeremiah is why we stay strong when we want to crumble. This promise is the reason we find the courage to get up, wipe off the dirt, and try again when we fall. Reread the verse out loud.

God created beautiful plans for your life. He knows every detail of your future, something your parents don't even know. God's plans for you are filled with good things and hard things, and both will give you a sense of hope if you let them.

Be brave, courageous girl. Don't allow tough times to steal your joy or kill your confidence, because God is with you, walking out every single day of life with you. Anything you face has to be approved by Him, so trust that if He has allowed it, there is a very good reason for it.

....

God, thank You for knowing my future.
Give me the courage to walk it out.

Day 49

Thankful for Care

In everything give thanks.
1 THESSALONIANS 5:18

I will never forget a time when Jodi was really little, maybe five years old, and she was sick in the middle of the night. Isn't that the worst—to wake up, feel awful and exhausted, and have to run to the restroom? Ugh! Jodi was throwing up again and again. I woke up too and was with her, getting washcloths and water, cleaning up, and doing what I could to make her feel better. She felt so terribly sick, yet in the midst of her sickness and pain she paused for a moment and said to me, "Mommy, thank you for taking care of me."

My eyes instantly filled with tears as my heart swelled with such great love for my little girl who thought to thank me even though she was sick and hurting. I encouraged her and wanted to bless her so much for showing that kind of gratitude!

I thought later about how much God as our heavenly Father must appreciate us and want to bless us when we thank Him for how He helps us even when we are going through a really hard time.

No matter what you might be struggling with, thank the people who are helping you, and more importantly, thank God, who works in and through people to help you. Every bit of love and care you receive ultimately comes from Him!

....

Dear God, in all kinds of situations,
thank You for always taking care of me. Amen.

Day 50

An Invitation to Be Brave

Where can I go from Your Spirit? Or where can I run away from where You are? If I go up to heaven, You are there! If I make my bed in the place of the dead, You are there! If I take the wings of the morning or live in the farthest part of the sea, even there Your hand will lead me and Your right hand will hold me.
Psalm 139:7–10

This verse is an invitation to be brave no matter what scary and hard things you are facing right now. The writer is sharing with you a reminder that God is always with you, and there is nowhere you can hide from Him. He sees everything that scares you and knows what makes you worry. He sees every tear that falls down your cheek. He knows the thoughts that make you doubt yourself. And because God loves you so much, He promises to be close to you and never leave your side.

Simply put, no matter if you're in good times or hard times, God is there to lead you and hold you.

God, because of You, I am brave. Thank You!

Day 51

Don't Stay Away

*Let us not stay away from church meetings.
Some people are doing this all the time. Comfort each
other as you see the day of His return coming near.*
HEBREWS 10:25

We often think of church as just a building we go to, when really the church is a group of people—all followers of Jesus Christ all around the world! But since we can't all meet in the same place at once, we do have buildings all over the place to meet together.

What is your favorite thing about your church? When I asked Jodi and Lilly this question, Jodi said learning more about God and the Bible, and Lilly said being with friends. Both of those are wonderful reasons to love time at church! We always need to keep learning more about God and His Word, and we need time with other people who love and want to worship God—that's called fellowship with other believers. It's so good to be together, to comfort and encourage each other, to learn together and sing and pray to God together. In fact, the Bible tells us not to stay away from church meetings in Hebrews 10:25!

There are so many types and styles of churches, but the most important thing about any of them is that they must preach the *whole* Word of God and do what it says—and glorify God by doing so. You glorify God by being part of a church like that! And you also learn and grow in prayer at church. A lot of things in life will tempt you to stop going to church, but don't ever stay away!

. . . .

*Dear God, thank You for Your church. Help me
to be active in it my whole life! Amen.*

Day 52

Have the Guts to Ask God

Those who are right with the Lord cry, and He hears them. And He takes them from all their troubles. The Lord is near to those who have a broken heart. And He saves those who are broken in spirit.
PSALM 34:17-18

Do you ever think your problems are too small to bring to God? With all the mess, muck, and mire in the world today, do you think God is too busy to hear you? Maybe you've decided He only wants to hear the big problems, not the everyday hurts and frustrations you're facing right now. But know this: that couldn't be further from the truth.

God has the supernatural ability to hear from everyone at the same time and give them His full attention. He can multitask like a pro. God delights in every part of you—the good, the bad, and everything in between. He wants to hear from you. And whether it's something big or something small, it all matters to Him. Because *you* matter to Him.

....

God, give me the guts to ask for Your help in all things. I love that You love me so much.

Day 53

All Five Fingers

Pray for all people.
1 TIMOTHY 2:1 NLT

When you were younger and learning to add, did you sometimes use your fingers? And then you started learning you shouldn't use your fingers because you could do it in your head! Lilly learned at church about a cool way to help focus your prayers—and you do get to use your fingers! It's called the five-finger prayer method. Maybe you've heard of it before, and if you google it, you'll find out more about it and different variations of it.

Basically, you use your hand to help guide your prayers to God for others. Your thumb, which is closest to your body, can remind you to pray for the people in your life who are closest to you. Your pointer finger can remind you to pray for people who point and direct others to learning and to help, like teachers, doctors, nurses, police officers, rescue workers, and those who are our elders. Your next finger, the tallest, can remind you to pray for leaders in our nation and our world, like the president and government workers and military personnel and business owners. The ring finger, which is the weakest, can remind you to pray for people who are weak and in trouble and pain and sickness in the world. And finally, your smallest finger can remind you to pray for your own needs.

Dear God, I pray for all people. We all need Your help with everything. Thank You for being Lord and Savior. Amen.

Day 54

Fearless Faith

Our life is lived by faith. We do not live by what we see in front of us.
2 CORINTHIANS 5:7

Sometimes it would be easier to trust God if we could see Him. If we could talk face-to-face and see His expressions, it would make God more real. Or if we could literally crawl up onto His lap and be comforted, it would strengthen our belief. It's hard not to see God, isn't it?

While you may not see His face before you go to heaven, you've most certainly seen His handiwork. Think about it. Has God fixed something you asked Him to? Did He heal someone? Did an impossible situation work out in your favor? Did you overcome fear and have a burst of courage to speak up? Did you ace the test? Did you make friends? Did you have the confidence to try something new?

All of those times are faith builders. They're reminders that you don't have to see God's face to trust Him. And when you're feeling weak or scared, just ask Him for fearless faith.

....

God, I don't need to see You to believe in You. I love You!

Real Friendship

Come close to God and He will come close to you.
JAMES 4:8

Have you ever met a new friend at a park or event or activity you're doing and you really liked hanging out with them, but then that time was over and you didn't get to spend time with them again? Even if you thought the new friend was great, you don't really have much of a friendship, do you? Real friendship takes time and effort. Sometimes people call Jesus their friend because they heard about Him and maybe spent a nice little time with Him at church, but then they don't really work on the relationship with Him. That's so sad, because He is always available through His Holy Spirit and His Word, the Bible. He always wants to grow closer to each of us, and He is the very best friend ever!

Each one of us must put time and effort into our relationship with Jesus. He is the Savior of everyone who believes in Him, but He doesn't want to be a distant Savior we meet once and never hang out with again. He wants to be the closest kind of BFF! We grow closer to Jesus by regularly spending time reading the Bible, going to a Bible-teaching church, serving others in Jesus' name, and praying to Him all the time.

....

Dear God, I want You as my very best friend,
and I want to spend time with You every single day.
Thank You for always being there for me! Amen.

Day 56

Overcoming the What-Ifs

*But the Lord has been my strong place,
my God, and the rock where I am safe.*
PSALM 94:22

Feeling safe and secure is a basic human need. Life can often make us nervous or fearful because it's unpredictable. No matter how hard we try to control everything, we just can't always know what tomorrow will bring, and it sometimes feels too big and scary.

Do you live in the what-ifs?

- What if I try and fail?
- What if they don't like me?
- What if I embarrass myself?
- What if I trust people and they let me down?

God uses scripture like Psalm 94:22 to remind you that He will be your safe place. With Him, the what-ifs lose their power because He promises to give you strength when you need it. Your job is to be bold enough to trust that God is for you and will help you every time you ask.

God, I need You to smash the what-ifs that keep me from trusting You. Help me to be bolder and more confident in You than in the things that scare me.

Day 57

Serving Jesus by Serving Others

"'I was hungry and you gave Me food to eat. I was thirsty and you gave Me water to drink. I was a stranger and you gave Me a room. I had no clothes and you gave Me clothes to wear. I was sick and you cared for Me. I was in prison and you came to see Me.' Then those that are right with God will say, 'Lord, when did we see You hungry and feed You? When did we see You thirsty and give You a drink? When did we see You a stranger and give You a room? When did we see You had no clothes and we gave You clothes? And when did we see You sick or in prison and we came to You?' Then the King will say, 'For sure, I tell you, because you did it to one of the least of My brothers, you have done it to Me.'"
MATTHEW 25:35–40

Reading God's Word in daily devotion time, praying constantly, worshipping God, and learning at church are all ways we grow in our relationship with Jesus. And the above scripture shows us exactly how to be close to Jesus. We serve Him directly when we feed the hungry, give water to the thirsty, share clothes with the needy, and visit those who are sick or imprisoned. Let yourself grow closer to Jesus by serving others in need. Pray for God to show you many opportunities for service all of your life!

Dear God, I want to serve You and draw close to You by serving others. Show me who, where, when, and how. Amen.

Are You a Drama Queen?

God is our safe place and our strength. He is always our help when we are in trouble. So we will not be afraid, even if the earth is shaken and the mountains fall into the center of the sea, and even if its waters go wild with storm and the mountains shake with its action.
PSALM 46:1–3

The psalmist is trying to calm our anxious heart and remind us that even if the worst scenario happens, God is with us. So often, we go negative in our thoughts. . . .

When you're in a fight with your friend, you're sure you two will never make up. When you fail a test, you decide you'll never pass your grade. When you disappoint your parents, you're afraid they'll never trust you again. Let's admit that sometimes we can all be drama queens. Amen?

What if you decided to be gutsy and retrain those drama-queen behaviors? Rather than take the crazy train to worst-scenario land, what if you prayed to God about what's bothering you? Rather than freak out, try asking for courage, strength, peace, or whatever you need.

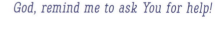

God, remind me to ask You for help!

Day 59

Praise God for Creation

For in six days the Lord made the heavens, the earth, the sea and all that is in them. And He rested on the seventh day.
Exodus 20:11

Think of your favorite amusement park and all the fun rides. Or what's your favorite city to visit? We love to travel and to go on amusement park rides, and we appreciate all the cool things about big cities. What God made people capable of designing and building is pretty amazing. None of it compares with the beauty and awesomeness of His creation, though! I went to Yellowstone National Park once, just for a day. (It wasn't nearly long enough, and I can't wait to go back!) I called it God's amusement park because there were so many different attractions all in one place, just like at an amusement park, and yet they were all fascinating natural wonders that no person could ever come close to creating. Only God can create supercool natural wonders!

What is your favorite national park or aspect of God's creation? When you're visiting it or looking at pictures you took when you were there in the past, spend time in prayer, thanking God and praising Him for making such beauty for us to appreciate!

....

Dear God, You are so awesome to have created such a beautiful world for us to live and grow in. Draw me closer to You as I appreciate everything You have made. Amen.

Day 60

The Nerve to Be Strong

Be happy in your hope. Do not give up when trouble comes. Do not let anything stop you from praying.
ROMANS 12:12

Sometimes being strong is the last thing you want to be. You'd rather hide under your covers or eat a tub of ice cream or binge-watch your favorite Netflix show. It takes real guts and determination to put on your big-girl pants and be brave.

Where do you need to be strong right now? Do you need to stand up for yourself or stand up for someone else? Is there a tough circumstance you have to walk through? Are you dealing with a hard family situation? Maybe you need to find the courage to fess up to something you've done.

According to Romans 12:12, you can choose to be full of hope for a good outcome. You can dig deep for the strength to not give up, and you can find the motivation to pray through it all. Today, choose to believe this and to walk it out every day.

....

God, will You give me the nerve to be strong so I can face the hard times?

Day 61

Look Inside

But the Lord said to Samuel, "Do not look at the way he looks on the outside or how tall he is, because I have not chosen him. For the Lord does not look at the things man looks at. A man looks at the outside of a person, but the Lord looks at the heart."
1 SAMUEL 16:7

God began by making one man. From him came all the different people who live everywhere in the world.

One of my favorite things about traveling and being in airports is the opportunity to people watch. While waiting for flights, I love to sit and observe all the different people and personalities coming and going in one place. Our amazing Creator God has made people so beautiful and unique, all with different features and shades of skin. But because of sin, people treating other people unequally and unfairly because of appearance or skin color is an ongoing problem in our world.

God loves for us to overcome this kind of sin by reaching out and showing kindness and love to others no matter what anyone looks like! As followers of Jesus, we should be praying constantly for people everywhere to appreciate all shades of skin and all types of appearances and to treat each other equally and respectfully, with kindness and compassion. People tend to look at the outward appearance, but God looks at our hearts (1 Samuel 16:7), and so should we!

Dear God, please help me to look at people like You do, seeing their hearts and not their outward appearances. You made and love each individual person, and You want me to show Your love to them too. Amen.

Day 62

God Is Bigger

*What can we say about all these things?
Since God is for us, who can be against us?*
ROMANS 8:31

Does it ever feel like the whole world is against you? You and your friends are fighting for silly reasons. Your teacher doesn't seem to like you or want you to succeed. Your coach cut your play time in half and you're not sure why. You get in trouble with your parents for the littlest things. Your siblings are acting especially mean. And everywhere you turn, it feels like people dislike you.

Believe it or not, those kinds of feelings are normal. Life can be hard, and it can make us feel all alone. Our problems can look like giants, making us feel like ants next to them. But God is for us. And that means nothing can run us over because He will always protect us.

Yes, you will have troubles and problems. But God is bigger and will give you the courage to face anything life throws at you.

....

*God, I'm so glad You are for me.
Please give me confidence and strength.*

Hearing without Listening

Come and listen, all you who fear God, and I will tell you what he did for me. For I cried out to him for help, praising him as I spoke. If I had not confessed the sin in my heart, the Lord would not have listened. But God did listen! He paid attention to my prayer. Praise God, who did not ignore my prayer or withdraw his unfailing love from me.
PSALM 66:16–20 NLT

Do you ever hear something but not really listen? We all do this, unfortunately. Sometimes if you're sitting in school, you can hear the teacher talking but you're not actually paying attention to what she's saying. Or maybe you heard your parents give you instructions or reminders but you didn't focus and follow through. We've all been there!

God always hears our prayers because He is omniscient and knows and sees all. But sometimes He doesn't seem to pay attention to them. Why is that? Sometimes it's because we are holding on to sins in our lives rather than admitting them to God and asking for His help to get rid of them. Because of Jesus, we can admit all our sins, ask forgiveness, and be free of them—and when we do, God pays attention to our prayers.

. . . .

Dear God, thank You for providing Jesus to free me from my sin. I admit and confess my sin to You. Thank You for taking it away. Thank You for paying attention to my prayers. Amen.

Day 64

Filling in the Gaps

"For God can do all things."
LUKE 1:37

On your own, your strength to handle problems is limited. You can only deal with so much friend drama. There is an end to your patience with that classmate who loves to annoy you. And your sibling only gets so much grace from you before things get ugly. Yes, you have limits.

But you also have a secret weapon that's available whenever you need it. God is ready to fill in the gaps that need filling. He didn't create you to be able to handle everything on your own. He gave you parents and friends to support you. But He also promises to be there whenever you need His help.

What feels like it's too much right now? Where are you struggling to hold it together? Where can't you figure things out? Who is hard to love right now?

When you're feeling like you don't have the courage and strength to take one more step, ask God for help.

....

God, I can't do this on my own.
Will You please fill in the gaps for me?

Day 65

Copycat

"When you stand to pray, if you have anything against anyone, forgive him. Then your Father in heaven will forgive your sins also. If you do not forgive them their sins, your Father in heaven will not forgive your sins."
MARK 11:25–26

When we're praying and want God to pay attention, we need God's forgiveness of our sins. And we also need to forgive others for the sins they have done that have hurt us. This is so important. God loves giving grace and forgiveness, and He wants us to do it too. Being a copycat of God and His good ways is wonderful! We should be so grateful for forgiveness of all our own sin that we want to give forgiveness generously to others just like God does.

This can be *sooo* very hard to do. Think of a time when someone was mean toward you and made you mad and hurt your feelings so much! Ugh, it's awful! But with God's power working in you, offering forgiveness is always possible. Even if someone who has hurt you doesn't ever seem sorry and you might never be close friends, you can still ask God to help you let go of the anger and pain they caused and trust that He is working all things out for good.

Dear God, I need Your help to copy forgiveness the way You give it so kindly and so generously. Please help me with this all the time! Amen.

Day 66

Fear vs. Trust

*When I am afraid, I will trust in You. I praise the
Word of God. I have put my trust in God. I will not
be afraid. What can only a man do to me?*
PSALM 56:3–4

Every day you have tons of choices to make. What cute outfit will you wear? Who will you sit by at lunch? What games will you play at recess? Will you do homework or watch television after school? But one of the most important choices you get to make is whether you will be afraid or whether you will trust God.

Just like choices, there are tons of opportunities each day to be scared. Think for a minute about what scared you today or yesterday. What made you worry? Where did you feel anxious? Did a concern keep you awake last night? Chances are you found a few fears tucked away in your day.

But there's good news! If you talk to God about those fears, you can know for sure He will help. So when fear pops up again, you can choose to trust He is already working on it.

....

*God, help me to trust You rather
than to fear something else.*

Day 67

Before You Even Ask

"Your Father knows what you need before you ask Him."
MATTHEW 6:8

If God knows what we need before we even ask Him, like Matthew 6:8 says, then you might wonder, *Why should I even pray at all? God already knows!*

And the answer is because God loves you that much! He wants a close relationship with you that much. He wants to hear from you even though He already knows everything about you and everything you need! Wow, that's the God of the whole universe wanting to be close to you. Amazing! The fact that He already knows everything about you plus everything about *everything* is a reason to want to talk to Him all the more, never a reason to think you don't need to bother praying!

....

Dear God, You are my good and loving Father. You know everything, and You already know exactly what I need in every situation. I am amazed by Your greatness and that You want to be close to me. Thank You! Amen.

Day 68

What Matters Most

"Gather together riches in heaven where they will not be eaten by bugs or become rusted. Men cannot break in and steal them. For wherever your riches are, your heart will be there also."
MATTHEW 6:20–21

Today's verse is a warning of sorts. It asks us to peek into ourselves and consider what is the most important thing to us. We may say it's God or church or family, but is it really? Think about what gets the majority of your time. Instagram? Friends? Video games or Netflix? Sports or books? Makeup or fashion?

The hard truth is that whatever gets your attention the very most is what you value the very most. It's hard to say no to friends because you need to spend time reading the Bible instead or to skip the premiere of your favorite television show because you planned to spend time journaling your prayers to God. But when you have the courage to invest in your relationship with God, it makes all the difference in your day.

....

God, my heart is with You. Give me the determination I need to make You number one in my life.

Don't Be a Show-Off

"When you pray, do not be as those who pretend to be someone they are not. They love to stand and pray in the places of worship or in the streets so people can see them. For sure, I tell you, they have all the reward they are going to get. When you pray, go into a room by yourself. After you have shut the door, pray to your Father Who is in secret. Then your Father Who sees in secret will reward you."
MATTHEW 6:5–6

You've probably encountered show-offs in your life, people who talk mostly about themselves and try to keep all the attention on themselves alone. Jesus talked about these kinds of people who even use prayer to show off. And He said not to be like them. Our prayers should be a sincere conversation with our heavenly Father, a time of praising Him and asking for His help.

Does this scripture passage mean that every single prayer we pray should be said in secret, when we're alone? No, but it is making the point that prayer should be sincere and only to our one true God and that in every prayer, we should want all attention on Him and His power alone, not on ourselves.

Dear God, help me never to want to put attention on myself in prayer but to put all attention on You. You are the only one worthy of receiving prayer and praise. Amen.

Day 70

Giving UP the Need to Control

Be quiet and know that I am God. I will be honored among the nations. I will be honored in the earth.
Psalm 46:10

Wanting to be in control is part of being human. Everyone, at least on some level, wants to be in control of things around them because it makes them feel safer. Can you relate?

What are the things you try to control? Maybe you are the leader of your group of friends or the captain of the team because you like to make decisions. Maybe you boss around your little brother or sister because you're certain you know better. Maybe you don't listen to suggestions because you want to choose for yourself. Where are you playing God in your life?

Today's verse is so good and true. It's a powerful reminder that God is God. . .and we are not. And since we often crave being in control, choosing to let God lead is a very brave decision.

You can still be a leader, but let God show you the way.

....

God, I give You control of my life. Give me the courage to follow You.

Day 71

Keep On Asking

Jesus said to them, "If one of you has a friend and goes to him in the night and says, 'Friend, give me three loaves of bread, for a friend of mine is on a trip and has stopped at my house. I have no food to give him.' The man inside the house will say, 'Do not trouble me. The door is shut. My children and I are in bed. I cannot get up and give you bread.' I say to you, he may not get up and give him bread because he is a friend. Yet, if he keeps on asking, he will get up and give him as much as he needs. I say to you, ask, and what you ask for will be given to you. Look, and what you are looking for you will find. Knock, and the door you are knocking on will be opened to you. For everyone who asks, will receive what he asks for. Everyone who looks, will find what he is looking for. Everyone who knocks, will have the door opened to him."
Luke 11:5–10

Do you wonder if God ever gets tired of you asking for things in prayer? Jesus Himself taught in the Bible that God absolutely does not! What a good Father! Do your parents ever get tired of you asking for things? Of course they do! No human parent could ever say they don't get annoyed sometimes by their children's repeated requests. But God is your all-powerful, never-tiring heavenly Father, and in Luke 11, Jesus tells you to keep on asking!

Dear God, thank You for never getting tired of my requests. I will keep on telling them to You! Amen.

Day 72

Praying the Gritty Prayers

You must keep praying. Keep watching! Be thankful always.
COLOSSIANS 4:2

Prayer is a powerful weapon when it feels like everything around you is crumbling. It keeps you focused on Jesus rather than on the struggles you're facing. When you pray, you are calling heaven down to earth, asking for God to help out in a situation. There's no doubt that prayer is one of the most effective weapons you have.

What does prayer look like in your life?

Today's verse tells us to keep praying. It's a clue for you. It's a cue to not give up in prayer. Sometimes we think that asking once is all we need. While that can be true, most of the time we need to pray whenever God brings a person or situation to mind. Why? It's not because God needs reminding. It's because it gives us courage, strength, wisdom, peace, or whatever else we need to keep going.

So keep praying, courageous girl. God is listening.

....

God, give me the resolve to pray until my request is answered.

Day 73

Always Ready

If you do not have wisdom, ask God for it. He is always ready to give it to you and will never say you are wrong for asking. You must have faith as you ask Him. You must not doubt. Anyone who doubts is like a wave which is pushed around by the sea. Such a man will get nothing from the Lord.
JAMES 1:5–7

Sometimes we have to wait on God to give us what we ask for, but James 1:5 tells us something God is always ready to give us: wisdom! And we sure do need God's wisdom in this mixed-up world, where so much of what is popular in our culture goes against the good truth and guidance in God's Word. So every day—even every minute!—ask God to give you His wisdom. Have faith and don't doubt that He gives it to you. Then use that wisdom in every area of your life! You definitely don't want to be like someone pushed around by the sea. That totally sounds like you'd get seasick, and there could be sharks too—yikes! You want to be someone who is steadily guided by God.

Dear God, thank You for being so generous with wisdom. I need it every minute, and I'm asking You again now. I believe You give it and You guide me with it. Amen.

Day 74

God Is Always There

The Lord said, "I Myself will go with you. I will give you rest."
EXODUS 33:14

God is always with you. Sometimes we think He is only in church or shows up only at youth group. We decide He is with those who need Him the very most—ones who need Him more than we do. But your heavenly Father stays close to you every minute of every day.

That means in the moments you feel alone, you really aren't. God is right there with you. The times when you're facing hard decisions that are scary, God will show you the way. When you feel rejected by friends, God will comfort you. He sees every tear and knows every heartache. God sees your courage and bravery. And He chooses to be with you because He delights in who you are.

How does this truth make you feel? In what ways does it encourage and comfort you? How does it change your understanding of the relationship you have with God?

....

*God, I'm so glad to know You are always with me.
Your presence makes me feel brave,
and I love You with all my heart!*

Day 75

Loving to Learn

Show me Your ways, O Lord. Teach me Your paths. Lead me in Your truth and teach me. For You are the God Who saves me.
PSALM 25:4–5

You might love school or not so much. With any type of school, there are probably some things you like about it and some you don't. Whatever the case, do you think learning ends just after you graduate high school or college? It shouldn't! Every day of your life, now when you're a kid and later when you're all grown up, you can wake up asking God, "Will You please teach me today?" And in every situation, whether good or bad, you can ask, "God, what do You want me to learn from this?" And you can repeat those prayers all throughout your days.

You can let God teach you through your teachers and subjects and experiences at school and then later on in life at work or at home caring for your family and in your relationships with others. You can listen and learn from other people's experiences. You can read good books and glean information from trustworthy sources and seek out wisdom from others. Most importantly, you can keep learning from God's Word and sound teaching at church and from other believers who are strong in their faith and following Jesus.

Dear God, please help me to never, ever stop learning and loving to learn. You created my beautiful mind and made it capable of so much. Show me how to use it for Your glory. Amen.

You Are Beautiful Just the Way You Are

But the Lord said to Samuel, "Do not look at the way he looks on the outside or how tall he is, because I have not chosen him. For the Lord does not look at the things man looks at. A man looks at the outside of a person, but the Lord looks at the heart."
1 SAMUEL 16:7

It's very hard to be confident in how you look, especially in today's world. Feeling good about who you are isn't easy.

We see ads on television or in magazines featuring girls we don't look like but wish we did. Instagram fills our heads with what society says is beautiful, and it makes us feel not good enough. The world's ideas of beauty set us up to feel unlovable.

But God reminds us of what's truly important: the heart. Find the courage to focus on being kind and generous and loving rather than focusing solely on what's on the outside. Yes, you are beautiful, just the way you are.

....

God, help me to be confident in who I am. And help me to love the way You made me!

Schooltime Prayer

The fear of the Lord is the beginning of much learning.
PROVERBS 1:7

At school you have a lot of opportunities to learn and you have a lot of opportunities to pray too! You might hear talk in the news about prayer being taken out of school, but it can never really be taken out if God's people are there! Any believer can pray silently at any time for God to help in any school situation. You can pray for teachers and staff. You can pray for your classmates. You can pray for opportunities to share God's love. You can pray for God to help you focus and do your best on tests and projects. You can pray for good relationships with classmates and teachers. You can pray for peace and safety at your school. And on and on! No one can ever stop you from silent prayer. Make your school and everything about it a big priority in your prayers, and watch how God works!

....

Dear God, I need Your help at school every day in a zillion ways. May I never stop asking for Your love and care. Amen.

Nope, Nothing

For I know that nothing can keep us from the love of God. Death cannot! Life cannot! Angels cannot! Leaders cannot! Any other power cannot! Hard things now or in the future cannot! The world above or the world below cannot! Any other living thing cannot keep us away from the love of God which is ours through Christ Jesus our Lord.
Romans 8:38-39

Think for a minute. What are the things you could do or the words you could speak that would cause God to turn His back on you? Think about the most trouble you've gotten into, or the snarkiest comment you've made to your mom, or the meanest thing you have done to your best friend. Do you believe any of those made God walk away?

Here's the truth: Just like today's verses say, there is nothing—*nothing*—that can keep you from God's love. You simply cannot do or say anything that will cause God to walk away from you. In a world where things change all the time, His love never does. It's rock solid.

God, help me to face the truth that Your love is forever and for always!

Day 79

Wait Time = Prayer Time

Wait for the Lord. Be strong. Let your heart be strong. Yes, wait for the Lord.
PSALM 27:14

Sometimes you might be waiting on a big change in your life or help for a big decision, and it seems like nothing is happening. But God might be doing a lot of work behind the scenes you have no idea about. So turn your wait times into extra special prayer times. Ask God to show you, little by little, His plans and His purposes. You might be amazed what He lets you see! And He might answer that He won't show you exactly what He's doing in your wait times, but you can pray for more trust in Him even when you can't see what He's doing.

Do you ever get frustrated that your parents don't always tell you what's going on or keep quiet about something they say you don't need to know about right now? Often their silence is for your own good—or maybe even for a wonderful surprise! Even more than your earthly parents, your heavenly Father is always working for your good, whether you understand wait times or not. And you can always praise Him with gratitude for simply being His child.

....

Dear God, it's hard to wait and not know exactly how You might be working behind the scenes. But I trust You and love You, and I'm so thankful I am Yours. Amen.

Day 80

Putting On a Brave Face

*This is the day that the Lord has made.
Let us be full of joy and be glad in it.*
PSALM 118:24

Sometimes you have to put on a brave face in the world. Maybe the day before was awful and you would rather hide in a hole than leave the comfort of your bed. Maybe life has been tough lately because your family is going through a divorce or you've lost someone to an illness. It takes real determination to go about your day when you are sad or discouraged.

But God created today, and He decided to have you be a part of it. He wanted you here. He made sure your eyes opened this morning. And even though you may be in a mess, you can choose to be full of joy anyway.

No, you don't have to be happy that life is super hard right now. That's not realistic. But you *can* choose to find joy in other places. Take a minute to name a few of those things right now.

....

God, I want to be joyful even when life is hard. Will You help me to do that?

Pray for Comfort and to Be a Comforter

We give thanks to the God and Father of our Lord Jesus Christ. He is our Father Who shows us loving-kindness and our God Who gives us comfort. He gives us comfort in all our troubles. Then we can comfort other people who have the same troubles. We give the same kind of comfort God gives us.
2 CORINTHIANS 1:3-4

In our little family, we love to get comfy and watch movies or read together, all snuggled up in soft blankets. Our dogs, Jasper and Daisy, love to snuggle in with us too. It's so comforting and relaxing to just be together. And sometimes we need extra comfort when we're experiencing the really hard and sad things of life.

What is your favorite kind of comfort? Whatever it is, remember that all good comfort comes from God, like 2 Corinthians 1 teaches us. The comfort you need might be through warm blankets and time with family. It might be an encouraging conversation with a friend or your favorite food cooked for you by Grandma when you're sick. It might be some extra special alone time with God and His Word speaking directly to your circumstances. And in times when you see others needing comfort, you can remember all that you've received and then be a giver of comfort too!

All the time, you can pray and ask your comforting Father in heaven for whatever comfort you need. And as you see Him answer and provide, ask Him to help you share comfort with others at every opportunity!

Dear God, I thank You so much for all the comfort You provide. Help me to share it generously! Amen.

Day 82

Peace and Strength

The peace of God is much greater than the human mind can understand. This peace will keep your hearts and minds through Christ Jesus.
PHILIPPIANS 4:7

What makes you feel peaceful? Is it hanging out with your friends or curling up for family movie night? Is it a hot bath complete with bubbles and a face mask? Maybe it comes from listening to music, journaling, or reading a good book. All of these are good! Finding freedom from life's yuckies is good for our heart and our health.

But even with these good options, the best peace you can ever have is the peace you get from Jesus. Have you ever asked Him for it? He offers the kind of peace that doesn't make any sense to others, because they'd be freaking out if they were in your shoes. His peace will help you get through anything.

When you can't find courage to get through your day. . .when you don't feel strong enough. . .when you're scared—pray for God to fill you with His peace.

. . . .

God, would You bring peace and comfort to me right now?

Day 83

Watch and Pray

"Watch and pray so that you will not be tempted. Man's spirit is willing, but the body does not have the power to do it."
MATTHEW 26:41

Sometimes we have the very best plans to do a good job with something, and then we just don't follow through. Do you ever plan to keep your room clean without being asked, but then two weeks later you can barely walk across the floor because toys and clothes and projects have piled up? Do you ever plan to study hard and long for an upcoming test but then find yourself quickly cramming the night before? Do you ever plan to have regular quiet time with God and His Word but you keep letting the busyness of the day get in the way?

We are human, and we have struggles and temptations that keep us from doing good. That's why we need to pray for God to help us. We need to tell Him, "I can't do this on my own! Because of sin, I'm tempted to mess up all the time! I need Your great big power working in me to overcome this temptation."

. . . .

Dear God, I sure do need Your great big power working in me to help with my struggles and temptations. I can't do anything good without You! Please help me with everything! Amen.

Day 84

The Courage to Step Out

Jesus said, "Come!" Peter got out of the boat and walked on the water to Jesus. But when he saw the strong wind, he was afraid. He began to go down in the water. He cried out, "Lord, save me!"
MATTHEW 14:29–30

Can you imagine the courage it took for Peter to leave the safety of the boat and step out onto the water where gravity would pull him down? You may not have been asked to do what Jesus asked of Peter, but can you remember a time it took every bit of courage to do something hard or scary?

Where is God asking you to be brave right now? What scares you the very most about it? What keeps you from trusting God enough to step out and do the next right thing?

When you need a big dose of courage, God is the one who will give you the exact amount you need. You may try to figure it out on your own, you may pledge to be gutsy. . .but your bravery will never match His. And luckily, it doesn't have to.

....

God, I want to live fearlessly. Please help me to be brave!

Turn Worry into Prayer

"Do not worry."
MATTHEW 6:25

As we're writing this book, we're trying not to worry about some big changes we have coming for our family this fall. And because a couple of years ago we lost a very dear loved one very suddenly, sometimes we worry about losing another loved one or friend unexpectedly. It would be easy to get caught up in these worries, but as each worry pops into our heads, we try our best to turn it into a prayer.

Among many verses in the Bible that tell us not to worry or be afraid, we love to remember Jesus' words in John 14:27: "Peace I leave with you. My peace I give to you. I do not give peace to you as the world gives. Do not let your hearts be troubled or afraid." And Psalm 55:22 says, "Give all your cares to the Lord and He will give you strength. He will never let those who are right with Him be shaken."

We know every person and family has their own challenges and troubles to face, and it's super hard not to worry about them. But you can train your brain to take those worrisome thoughts and give them over to God in prayer.

....

Dear God, You know my every thought, and You know when those thoughts are worries that are bad for me. Worries steal my peace and trust in You. Please take each worry from my mind and replace it with a powerful and soothing truth about Your strength, Your protection, and Your love for me. Amen.

Dare to Rest

"Come to Me, all of you who work and have heavy loads. I will give you rest. Follow My teachings and learn from Me. I am gentle and do not have pride. You will have rest for your souls. For My way of carrying a load is easy and My load is not heavy."
MATTHEW 11:28–30

These days, our schedules are crazy. Between school, after-school stuff, youth group, and homework, we can barely find time to rest. We are so overscheduled and super overcommitted, and it leaves us exhausted. And while it leaves us physically tired, it also makes us tired emotionally. It takes a lot of mental energy to be so busy!

So. . .what do you do when you're worn out?

God invites you to take every bit of your exhaustion and give it to Him. He will restore your soul if you talk to Him about what's draining your energy. Ask God to give you much-needed rest today.

God, give me boldness to share with You the things that are wearing me out and draining my joy. Thank You for giving me rest in return.

Day 87

Always Pray and Never Give Up

Jesus told them a picture-story to show that men should always pray and not give up.
LUKE 18:1

Read and learn from in this passage:

> Jesus told them a picture-story to show that men should always pray and not give up. He said, "There was a man in one of the cities who was head of the court. His work was to say if a person was guilty or not. This man was not afraid of God. He did not respect any man. In that city there was a woman whose husband had died. She kept coming to him and saying, 'Help me! There is someone who is working against me.' For awhile he would not help her. Then he began to think, 'I am not afraid of God and I do not respect any man. But I will see that this woman whose husband has died gets her rights because I get tired of her coming all the time.'" Then the Lord said, "Listen to the words of the sinful man who is head of the court. Will not God make the things that are right come to His chosen people who cry day and night to Him? Will He wait a long time to help them? I tell you, He will be quick to help them. But when the Son of Man comes, will He find faith on the earth?" (Luke 18:1–8)

....

Dear God, if people who don't even respect You choose to help make things right for those who ask them, how much more do You, my all-powerful, all-loving Father want to help me? Thank You so much! Amen.

Day 88

Do You Have the Guts to Wait?

I wait for the Lord. My soul waits and I hope in His Word.
PSALM 130:5

Waiting for God's answers is a gutsy choice because waiting is definitely one of the hardest things to do! We live in a "microwave society." We're used to getting what we want quickly.

Think about it. Have you been annoyed by a fast-food restaurant line moving too slowly? Or frustrated because the teacher didn't grade your test quickly? Maybe your parents didn't give you an answer about a party right when you wanted it or your friend didn't text you back within seconds, and it annoyed you.

When you wait for the Lord, it helps build your faith. And because waiting is and will always be a part of life, learning to wait well will bless you and grow your trust in God. He sees you. He knows the answers you need. And courageous girl, He is working on your behalf. So find the grit to wait for God to show you the next right step.

. . . .

God, please give me peace and confidence that You're working everything out for my good.

Day 89

Let Creation Encourage You

*"But ask the wild animals, and they will teach you.
Ask the birds of the heavens, and let them tell
you. Or speak to the earth, and let it teach you.
Let the fish of the sea make it known to you.
Who among all these does not know that the hand
of the Lord has done this? In His hand is the life
of every living thing and the breath of all men."*
JOB 12:7–10

Sometimes when I get discouraged about hard things in this world and all the bad things I hear and read in the news, I just need to get outside into God's creation. Looking at a giant tree that grew from a tiny seed or watching a magnificent sunset spread brilliant colors across the sky or listening to a bird sing a song that no other creatures sing—these all help put my heart and mind and prayers back in good perspective. I remember that all this beautiful creation came from nothing. God created and designed our world; He created and designed each plant and flower and creature; He created and designed each person in His image; and He created and designed a plan to save us and give us perfect eternal life with Him.

Dear God, thank You for encouraging me through all that You have made. Remind me every day of Your power and Your purposes. Help me to trust that You have the best plans. Amen.

Day 90

Ask in Boldness

And my God will give you everything you need because of His great riches in Christ Jesus.
PHILIPPIANS 4:19

Paul reminds us in this verse that God will make sure we have every single thing we need to survive and thrive in this life. Here's where that gets tricky. So often, what you *think* you need and what God *knows* you need are two different things.

You may decide that unless you make the team or make first chair in the band, you'll die. Or unless you get an invite to a certain birthday party, you just can't go on living. Of course not literally, but you get the point.

The truth is that God loves you too much to give you what you want when He knows what you really need. Your job is to ask in boldness and then trust His answer. So ask away! And remember, God will always respond in ways that are best for you!

God, You know the desires of my heart. You know what I am hoping for. Today I'm fearless asking for them, and I am determined to trust Your answer no matter what.

Lots from Just a Little: Part 1

Jesus looked up and saw many people coming to Him. He said to Philip, "Where can we buy bread to feed these people?" He said this to see what Philip would say. Jesus knew what He would do. Philip said to Him, "The money we have is not enough to buy bread to give each one a little." One of His followers was Andrew, Simon Peter's brother. He said to Jesus, "There is a boy here who has five loaves of barley bread and two small fish. What is that for so many people?" Jesus said, "Have the people sit down." There was much grass in that place. About five thousand men sat down.
JOHN 6:5–10

When I was a little girl, this account from John 6 was probably my favorite story in all the Bible, and it's still one of my favorites. I like to picture myself there that day. Can you picture it too? How generous of the boy to give up his lunch for Jesus. I wonder exactly what he was thinking when he did. I'll bet he never imagined the miracle Jesus was about to do with his lunch!

Dear Jesus, keep reminding me that You can do miracles with anything at all! Amen.

Day 92

Lots from Just a Little: Part 2

Jesus took the loaves and gave thanks. Then He gave the bread to those who were sitting down. The fish were given out the same way. The people had as much as they wanted. When they were filled, Jesus said to His followers, "Gather up the pieces that are left. None will be wasted." The followers gathered the pieces together. Twelve baskets were filled with pieces of barley bread. These were left after all the people had eaten. The people saw the powerful work Jesus had done. They said, "It is true! This is the One Who speaks for God Who is to come into the world."
JOHN 6:11–14

You might be young and feel like you don't have much to offer to Jesus. You might think only when you're a grown-up can Jesus do big things for His glory through you. But that's just not true. As you give your life to Jesus, pray to Him each day like this:

....

Dear Jesus, I am young and don't have big things to offer You, but I offer what I do have with my whole heart. I trust that You can turn what I have into much bigger things, according to Your will, to show Your love and glory. You are so incredibly amazing! Amen.

Don't Be a Worrywart

*Do not worry. Learn to pray about everything.
Give thanks to God as you ask Him for what you need.*
PHILIPPIANS 4:6

Take a moment and think of all the situations and people that cause you to worry. Maybe your grades are not what's expected of you. Maybe your parents have been fighting more than usual. Maybe a grandparent's health is starting to go downhill. Maybe tryouts are right around the corner. Maybe it's something completely out of your control.

God included this verse in the Bible because He knew you'd have a million reasons to worry. It's hard to live with confidence when we're so full of anxiety. Sometimes it seems like stress will never go away.

Prayer is an awesome way to get what's bothering you off your chest. God wants to hear from you, and He is available twenty-four hours a day, seven days a week. You can literally talk to Him at any time about anything. It may take some getting used to, but practice praying. It's a powerful habit to have!

*God, help me to stand up to worry by praying.
Thank You for always being available to me!*

Day 94

A Supernatural Transfer

The Lord God is my strength. He has made my feet like the feet of a deer, and He makes me walk on high places.
HABAKKUK 3:19

Have you ever seen a deer run in a field or dart up a hillside? They're sure-footed, which means they make it look effortless. Rather than be scared or nervous, they move with confidence because they know their bodies can do what is needed.

When you ask God to help you, you can have that same confidence because He promises to give you strength for what you're struggling with. You can access God's power to be bold and brave. It's a supernatural transfer from Him to you that gives you the guts to take the next step.

Where do you need God's strength right now? What are you facing that feels scary? Where do you need to find the courage to stand up for what's right? Spend time today talking to God about those places, and ask Him to help you be strong.

....

God, I know You will give me Your strength to face the hard times. Would You transfer it to me right now?

Day 95

Love and Prayer for Who?

You have heard people say, "Love your neighbors and hate your enemies." But I tell you to love your enemies and pray for anyone who mistreats you. Then you will be acting like your Father in heaven. He makes the sun rise on both good and bad people. And he sends rain for the ones who do right and for the ones who do wrong. If you love only those people who love you, will God reward you for this? Even tax collectors love their friends. If you greet only your friends, what's so great about this? Don't even unbelievers do that? But you must always act like your Father in heaven.
MATTHEW 5:43–48 CEV

This scripture is a great example of how God's ways are often so opposite of our world's ways. It's popular and easy to love just your friends and family and those who love you and to hate those who hate you. But that's not what God says to do, and it's sure not popular or easy to love and pray for the enemies and meanies in your life. Yet that's what God wants. It seems totally impossible sometimes! But with His help, you can do this, and so can we. It might be a huge struggle at first, but try it out and keep trying! Then watch how God blesses you when you obey His good commands and seek His help to love and pray for enemies.

....

Dear God, this good command of Yours is super hard to obey, and I sure can't do it on my own. But with Your help, I want to love and pray for my enemies. Amen.

Day 96

The Whole Enchilada

*"You will look for Me and find Me,
when you look for Me with all your heart."*
JEREMIAH 29:13

Sometimes we look for the shortcut or the easy way out. We want to do the least amount of work and get the very best results. We do the bare minimum and hope for an epic outcome. And while we may be halfhearted in some areas, God wants us to be wholehearted with Him.

What does that mean for you? It means He wants you to have a deep longing to be in a relationship with Him. Rather than just hearing from you at church on Sunday or in youth group, God wants to hear from you every day. He wants the whole enchilada, not just a bite.

Think about your bestie. You hang out at school, text and talk on the phone, and have tons of sleepovers. You share clothes and secrets and even finish each other's sentences. You want to be together all the time.

God wants you to have that same desire to be with Him. Choose to have an unwavering relationship with the one who created you!

....

God, I want You!

Filled with Love

I pray that you will be filled with love. I pray that you will be able to understand how wide and how long and how high and how deep His love is. I pray that you will know the love of Christ. His love goes beyond anything we can understand. I pray that you will be filled with God Himself.
Ephesians 3:17-19

So often, the troubled and mean people in our lives act terribly toward others because they have so little love in their own lives. So as you're praying for enemies, this prayer in Ephesians 3 is a wonderful one to focus on for them. Of course you can and should pray it for friends and loved ones too. But if you pray it for enemies, who knows how God might completely transform their hearts? They might even end up becoming good friends. What a miracle that would be! God can do anything!

. . . .

Dear God, please fill my enemies up to overflowing with Your love. Help me to show Your love to them however they need, however You want me to. Amen.

Day 98

God Is Smarter

"For as the heavens are higher than the earth, so are My ways higher than your ways, and My thoughts than your thoughts."
ISAIAH 55:9

You may be a straight-A student and on the honor roll. You may have scored the highest grade on a test or won the spelling bee. Maybe you're in advanced classes or you've been told you have wisdom beyond your years. Those are all huge accomplishments. Be proud of yourself! But God is still smarter, and that's a good thing.

God reminds us that He has endless knowledge and understanding about everything. While we only see part of the picture, He sees it from every angle. He knows why things happen and He knows how they'll turn out. He knows every single detail of your life—the good, the bad, and everything in between.

Because His ways and thoughts are higher than yours, choose to bravely trust Him. God has a hope and a future planned out for you, and while it may be bumpy at times, it will be good.

....

God, thank You for being smarter than I am! May I trust You instead of trying to figure it out myself.

Day 99

Pray Together

*"For where two or three are gathered together
in My name, there I am with them."*
MATTHEW 18:20

Every time I went to pick up Jodi from Sunday school at church last school year, my heart filled up with joy and encouragement when I peeked in the window on the door. I loved seeing the girls in her class standing in a circle, holding hands, eyes closed as they finished their time together. Jodi told me all the girls shared prayer requests and praises with their teachers and with each other and then took turns praying out loud about those needs and celebrations. What a blessing! And then they could remember to pray for their friends whenever they came to mind during the coming week. Knowing that others care about your needs and the things you're celebrating can be super encouraging.

Do you have friends or family members with whom you share requests and pray? I hope so! If not, start today by initiating a regular prayer time with your family. And at church or school or your activities, offer to pray for your friends, and ask them to pray for you too.

....

Dear God, thank You for family and friends and the times when we gather so we can all talk to You together! These times encourage me so much, and I want to make them a habit. Amen.

Day 100

Bold Declarations

*But I am like a green olive tree in the house of God.
I trust in the loving-kindness of God forever and ever.*
PSALM 52:8

What a bold declaration the psalmist makes here. He's putting on paper—for all to read—that he chooses to trust God's love for him, no matter what. That means all eyes will be watching to see if his statement stands up when struggles try to bring him down.

Could you make the same kind of declaration, knowing people may hold you to it?

Part of walking out your faith is being willing to stand up for it. It's being courageous and admitting that you're a Jesus girl. It's being strong even when others make fun of you for believing in God. It's not being afraid to pray in public or talk to your friends about Him.

If you ask, God will make you gutsy enough to be unashamed of your faith. It may be scary, but He will help you be fearless as you are honest about what He means in your life.

....

God, I want to be bold and confident in my faith and live it out loud! Give me courage!

Day 101

Turn Away

Turn away from what is sinful. Do what is good. Look for peace and follow it. The eyes of the Lord are on those who do what is right and good. His ears are open to their cry. The face of the Lord is against those who sin.
PSALM 34:14–16

The Bible is clear that to have good communication with God through our prayers, we have to keep ourselves away from what is sinful. If we've asked Jesus to be our Savior, then we are right with God because of His grace. But that doesn't mean we should purposefully choose to lie or cheat or do anything that goes against God's Word again and again.

Romans 5:20–6:2 (NLT) says, "God's law was given so that all people could see how sinful they were. But as people sinned more and more, God's wonderful grace became more abundant. So just as sin ruled over all people and brought them to death, now God's wonderful grace rules instead, giving us right standing with God and resulting in eternal life through Jesus Christ our Lord. Well then, should we keep on sinning so that God can show us more and more of his wonderful grace? Of course not!"

Dear God, I know that because Jesus is my Savior, You take away my sin. But even though I am saved, I don't want to purposefully go against Your Word. I love You and want to please You. Thank You for Your perfect grace. Amen.

Day 102

Live Untangled

Trust in the Lord with all your heart, and do not trust in your own understanding. Agree with Him in all your ways, and He will make your paths straight.
PROVERBS 3:5–6

It's so easy for life to get all tangled up, isn't it? You may start out on the straight and narrow—following rules, being kind, minding your own business, not letting others make you mad, doing your homework and chores—but sometimes it takes just one bad choice to mess it all up.

What do you do when life gets tangled? Do you talk to a friend or a parent? Maybe you drown your frustration in video games or in homemade cookies. Maybe you journal or listen to music. We all have ways to get through life's messes. But do you ever talk to God about it?

Why not ask God what He thinks about your tangles? Ask Him to help you see things like He does. Ask for courage to take the next right step. Then tell God you're going to trust He is working out the tangles in your favor.

....

God, would You please straighten out my tangles?

Day 103

Perfection

And if someone asks about your hope as a believer, always be ready to explain it. But do this in a gentle and respectful way. Keep your conscience clear. Then if people speak against you, they will be ashamed when they see what a good life you live because you belong to Christ.
1 PETER 3:15–16 NLT

If you and your life were absolutely perfect, what would that look like? Each unique person will have a different idea of this, and it's kind of fun to think about. It will never happen on this earth, though, so remember it's just a dream for now! Only in heaven will you be perfect and have perfect life forever. Only Jesus was a perfect human on this earth. Because of Him, you never have to worry about trying to be perfect or pretending to be perfect. If you've asked Him to be your Savior, then He is your perfection and you belong to Him.

The hope and perfection Jesus gives is something we should totally want to share with others, like the Bible tells us to. Ask God to help you be ready at any time to explain what it means to believe in and follow Jesus, always in a kind and respectful way. Ask Him to bring people into your life who need to hear about Him. And keep living such a good life in Jesus that no one can speak badly about you, even if they try!

....

Dear God, help me to be ready all the time to share with others about how perfect You are and why all my hope is in You to have a perfect forever! Amen

Dare to See the Good

My Christian brothers, you should be happy when you have all kinds of tests. You know these prove your faith. It helps you not to give up.
JAMES 1:2–3

This is hard! James isn't suggesting we be happy when difficult things come into our life; he is telling us we *need* to be. He is saying we should put on our big-girl pants and be brave—brave enough to trust that God is working in the mess. James is asking us to be fearless because it's an opportunity to strengthen our faith.

How do you feel about that? How does James's statement that you should be happy in the hard stuff challenge you today?

The truth is that God is 100 percent in control and knows exactly what you need. Even more, He only allows the yuckies because He'll use them for your benefit. The hard times will make you stronger, more compassionate, wiser, and braver. While we may not like being hurt, we can choose to be happy that on the other side of it will be something good.

....

God, give me the courage to get through the mess with a positive attitude.

Day 105

Pray to Be Like Jesus

Jesus was healing many people of all kinds of sickness and disease and was putting out demons. Many that were blind were able to see. Jesus said to John's followers, "Go back to John the Baptist and tell him what you have seen and heard. Tell him the blind are made to see. Those who could not walk, are walking. Those with a bad skin disease are healed. Those who could not hear, are hearing. The dead are raised to life and poor people have the Good News preached to them. The person who is not ashamed of Me and does not turn away from Me is happy."
LUKE 7:21-23

Jesus loved and cared for people like no other human ever has or ever will. He healed and provided for the sick and needy. He reached out to the lonely and unwanted. He taught truth and showed people the one and only way to God in heaven.

And if we are true followers of Jesus, then we will do these things too! What are the ways you and your family are doing that now? Or how could you start? Keep asking God how He wants you to care for the needs of others and help spread His truth and hope.

....

Dear God, please help me to give and to care and to share truth and hope. I want to truly love and reach out to people like Jesus did. Amen.

Godly Beauty

Your beauty should come from the inside. It should come from the heart. This is the kind that lasts. Your beauty should be a gentle and quiet spirit. In God's sight this is of great worth and no amount of money can buy it.
1 PETER 3:4

Beauty has been distorted by the world. The way we decide if someone is beautiful is often very different from how God does.

Think about ways you and your friends define beauty. Is it because of a girl's weight or the clothes she wears? Is it based on how long her hair is, its color, or how she styles it? Is someone pretty because of how she does her makeup? It's easy to look on the outside, isn't it?

But God says beauty comes from inside because it doesn't change with time or trends. Can you think of someone who is kind and compassionate? A girl who treats others well and makes smart choices? That's godly beauty, and *that* takes confidence and courage.

....

God, I want to be beautiful by Your definition!

Day 107

Special Holiday Prayers

Pray in the Spirit at all times and on every occasion. Stay alert and be persistent in your prayers for all believers everywhere.
EPHESIANS 6:18 NLT

Jodi and Lilly's grandma has oodles of cute decorations for every holiday, and they love to help her decorate her house for each of them. Holidays are all kinds of fun, providing great times for family and friends to get together for parties and gift giving and picnics and egg hunts! They are also special times that can help us remember to pray in special ways. Here are just a few ideas:

Christmas—Give special thanks to God for sending Jesus as a baby to live a human life like us and to be our Savior.

Easter—Sing to and praise God that Jesus rose from the dead and offers eternal life! Pray for all people to trust Him as Savior!

Memorial Day—Thank God for those who have given their lives in military service to help us live in freedom.

Fourth of July—Thank God for our nation and pray for protection and peace.

Thanksgiving—Thank God for how He provides and guides. Keep track of your blessings and spend time sharing them with loved ones, thanking God together.

....

Dear God, help me to remember that extra-special days, like holidays, are perfect times for extra-special prayers to You! Amen.

Day 108

Supergirl Strength

He answered me, "I am all you need. I give you My loving-favor. My power works best in weak people." I am happy to be weak and have troubles so I can have Christ's power in me.
2 CORINTHIANS 12:9

It doesn't feel good to fail at things, does it? No one likes to think they can't do something. When it gets hard, you want to raise your fist in the air and shout, "Girl power!" like a true superhero. But the truth is that because you are human, you don't have superpowers.

You do, however, have access to God's supernatural power. That means that when you don't have the strength or courage to take the next step, He will give you His. When you are too afraid to act, God's power will make you brave. When you need to do something that feels impossible, He will give you confidence.

....

God, I cannot do the hard things without You. I need Your awesome power right now!

Day 109

Birthday Blessings

Dear friend, I hope all is well with you.
3 John 1:2 nlt

On the birthdays of your friends and loved ones, you can pray extra special scripture prayers for the birthday girl or boy:

- "May the Lord bless you and protect you. May the Lord smile on you and be gracious to you. May the Lord show you his favor and give you his peace" (Numbers 6:24–26 nlt).

- "I pray that God, the source of hope, will fill you completely with joy and peace because you trust in him" (Romans 15:13 nlt).

- "I pray that God will make you ready to obey him and that you will always be eager to do right. May Jesus help you do what pleases God" (Hebrews 13:21 cev).

- "May our Lord Jesus Christ himself and God our Father. . . comfort you and strengthen you in every good thing you do and say" (2 Thessalonians 2:16–17 nlt).

Of course, you can pray and should pray these for yourself and anyone on *any* day.

Dear God, thank You for creating my family and friends and for the opportunities to celebrate their beautiful lives. Please bless them and help them in all ways, every day. Amen.

Day 110

Bravely Step Aside

*Yet I am always with You. You hold me by my right hand.
You will lead me by telling me what I should do.
And after this, You will bring me into shining-greatness.*
PSALM 73:23-24

Did you catch the words *and after this* in today's scripture? It's a reminder that something will happen first. It means that before the awesome thing comes, a hard or challenging thing must happen. And this passage of scripture lets us know that the requirement for the good thing was choosing to give up control and let God lead instead.

If you were to be honest, you'd probably admit that you like being in control. Who doesn't, right? When we are the ones making decisions, life feels easier. Better. It's nice to be the leader. But God wants to make sure you find the way to the shining-greatness.

He is trustworthy and wants the very best for you! And if you bravely step aside and ask God to lead your life, He will help you create something beautiful.

....

*God, I admit I like to be in control.
But I want what You have for me even more.*

Day 111

When It's Good to Feel Yucky

"When the Spirit of truth comes, he will guide you into all truth."
JOHN 16:13 NLT

Being carsick is such a yucky feeling! Lilly remembers a time she felt awful in the back of the car, but it didn't have anything to do with motion sickness. The yucky feeling was actually the good kind of yucky that helps us feel sorry for sin and want to make it right. The song "Live Alive" by Rend Collective was playing, and the lyrics about not wanting to "live a lie" reminded Lilly she should confess about a lie she had told. I looked in my rearview mirror and could see the tears on her face, and then she shared with me about the lie, told the truth instead, and said she was sorry to me and to God.

So what a blessing that yucky feeling actually was! We do feel yucky when we are holding on to sin and not confessing it to others and to God and asking for forgiveness. Because He loves us so much, God sometimes purposefully gives us yucky feelings inside through His Holy Spirit. Getting a yucky feeling as a reminder to confess sin is a whole lot better than letting lies and sin get bigger and bigger in our lives! As soon as Lilly confessed and received forgiveness, the yucky feeling was gone! We all should pray all the time for yucky feelings that help us admit our sins and make them right.

Dear God, please help me to choose to live by Your Word. But when I do mess up, I want to feel yucky about choosing to sin and holding on to it. Help me to admit and confess my sins and ask forgiveness quickly, every time. Thank You for Your grace! Amen.

Day 112

An Attitude of Gratitude

*Let us give thanks all the time to God through
Jesus Christ. Our gift to Him is to give thanks.
Our lips should always give thanks to His name.*
HEBREWS 13:15

Talk about manners! The writer here in Hebrews wants to make sure we know the importance of giving thanks to God. Within this twenty-nine-word scripture, he tells us three times to be thankful. And since God chose to include this verse in the Bible, it must really matter that we're grateful to Him. Even more, we're told to thank Him all the time because our praise is a gift.

It's easy to ask the Lord for all the things we want, but so often we forget to thank Him for what we have. We don't tell Him how happy we are for answered prayer.

Today, write down all the things God has done for you. Then spend time in prayer, thanking Him for those things. Be bold in your thankfulness and tell God how He helped so much. Create an attitude of gratitude to God every day.

....

*God, You're so good to me!
Thank You, thank You, thank You!*

Day 113

Relieved, Forgiven, and Free

*If we say we have not sinned, we are fooling ourselves,
and the truth isn't in our hearts. But if we confess our sins to God,
he can always be trusted to forgive us and take our sins away.*
1 JOHN 1:8–9 CEV

Even after we pray to confess sin and have asked forgiveness from God and those we've hurt, sometimes it's easy to keep feeling awful for what we did wrong. But God promises time and again in His Word that we never need to do that. He takes our sins far away—as far as the east is from the west, actually (Psalm 103:11–12)! If God is not holding on to them, why should we?

Our enemy, Satan, wants us to focus on our mistakes and beat ourselves up so that we keep feeling defeated and useless. So pray against the enemy and believe in the power of Jesus to forgive you and take your sin totally away!

. . . .

Dear God, You promise that when I confess my sins, You take them away and never remember them again. May I to hold on tightly to that truth. The enemy wants me to feel awful and trapped and defeated by sin, but when I confess my sin, You want me to feel relieved, forgiven, and free from it! I trust that You love and forgive perfectly and completely! Amen.

The Bad News Dare

He will not be afraid of bad news.
His heart is strong because he trusts in the Lord.
PSALM 112:7

Bad news is scary, that's for sure. From failing a test to discovering a friend's betrayal to learning your family is moving to another state, no one likes it when difficult news shows up. So how do you respond to it?

Some people get angry and throw a fit. Some cry themselves to sleep, become very sad, or bury their worries in a tub of ice cream. Others ignore it, avoid it, or refuse to believe it. But do you ever choose to trust God instead? What would that even look like?

Here is your bad-news dare: The next time something yucky happens, rather than freak out, tell God you trust Him. When sad news hits, ask God to make you courageous. Ask Him to calm your fearful heart and racing mind with His peace. Yes, there are a million reasons to be afraid of bad news, but with the Lord you don't have to be.

. . . .

God, I am choosing to trust in You rather than be afraid.

Day 115

Joined to the Vine

I am the true vine, and my Father is the gardener.
JOHN 15:1 CEV

Jesus used an example of a grapevine to show us how we can produce fruit—in other words, do good things in our lives for God's glory—and to help us understand how God answers our prayers:

> Stay joined to me, and I will stay joined to you. Just as a branch cannot produce fruit unless it stays joined to the vine, you cannot produce fruit unless you stay joined to me. I am the vine, and you are the branches. If you stay joined to me, and I stay joined to you, then you will produce lots of fruit. But you cannot do anything without me. If you don't stay joined to me, you will be thrown away. You will be like dry branches that are gathered up and burned in a fire. Stay joined to me and let my teachings become part of you. Then you can pray for whatever you want, and your prayer will be answered (John 15:4–7 CEV).

We must stay close to our Savior, following Him daily, reading His Word, obeying His commands so they become a part of us, spending time in prayer, and asking for His guidance in everything we do.

Dear God, help me to stay joined to Jesus.
That is the very best place to be. Amen.

Being Known

O Lord, You have looked through me and have known me. You know when I sit down and when I get up. You understand my thoughts from far away. You look over my path and my lying down. You know all my ways very well. Even before I speak a word, O Lord, You know it all.
PSALM 139:1–4

As girls, there is something wonderful about being known. Think about it. When friends surprise you with your favorite candy or grandparents give you gift cards to stores you love the most or Mom makes your favorite meal to celebrate your birthday, you feel important. How awesome for others to know the things that delight your heart! How amazing to be known. And how courageous to open yourself up enough for others to see the real you!

God knows you better than anyone ever could. He knows you better than you know yourself! Reread today's verses out loud and then thank Him for caring about you so much. And ask for the confidence to continue sharing yourself with others. You are worthy of knowing!

....

God, thank You for creating me. . . and for knowing me too!

Powerful Words: Part 1

No one can tame the tongue.
JAMES 3:8 NLT

The Bible talks strongly about the power of the tongue:

> We all make many mistakes. If there were a person who never said anything wrong, he would be perfect. He would be able to control his whole body, too. We put bits into the mouths of horses to make them obey us. We can control their whole bodies. It is the same with ships. A ship is very big, and it is pushed by strong winds. But a very small rudder controls that big ship. The man who controls the rudder decides where the ship will go. The ship goes where the man wants. It is the same with the tongue. It is a small part of the body, but it brags about doing great things.
>
> A big forest fire can be started with only a little flame. And the tongue is like a fire. It is a whole world of evil among the parts of our bodies. The tongue spreads its evil through the whole body. It starts a fire that influences all of life. The tongue gets this fire from hell. People can tame every kind of wild animal, bird, reptile, and fish, and they have tamed them. But no one can tame the tongue. (James 3:2–8 ICB)

We can do so much good with our words, or we can do damage. That's why we need to pray to have self-control over our tongues!

....

*Dear God, I need Your mighty power to
make me careful about what I say. Amen.*

Day 118

Powerful Words: Part 2

If you talk a lot, you are sure to sin. If you are wise, you will keep quiet.
PROVERBS 10:19 ICB

As we pray for self-control over our words, we can focus on and pray specific scriptures that teach us how to use our words in good, encouraging, wise, and helpful ways. Scriptures like these:

- "Let the teaching of Christ and His words keep on living in you. These make your lives rich and full of wisdom" (Colossians 3:16).

- "Watch your talk! No bad words should be coming from your mouth. Say what is good. Your words should help others grow as Christians" (Ephesians 4:29).

- "A gentle answer turns away anger, but a sharp word causes anger" (Proverbs 15:1).

- "Pleasing words are like honey. They are sweet to the soul and healing to the bones" (Proverbs 16:24).

- "He who watches over his mouth and his tongue keeps his soul from troubles" (Proverbs 21:23).

Dear God, "let the words of my mouth and the thoughts of my heart be pleasing in Your eyes, O Lord, my Rock and the One Who saves me" (Psalm 19:14).

She Will Not Be Moved

*God is in the center of her. She will not be moved.
God will help her when the morning comes.*
PSALM 46:5

This verse is talking about Jerusalem and how nothing could take it down because it was a holy city. Just like that city, you too are holy if you believe in Jesus, ask Him to be the Savior of your life, and call on His name. Let's personalize this verse, because it's a powerful reminder of the truth we live out every day as Jesus girls.

Every time you see the word *her* or *she* in today's scripture, replace it with your name. Speak this out loud a few times and declare it about your life.

Then on those days when you feel rejected or betrayed, when you feel like you're unlovable or not good enough, when you're worried that everything is going to crumble around you, read that verse out loud again with your name. God will not let you be taken down. Place your courage and confidence in Him.

. . . .

*God, You are in the center of me.
With Your strength, I am a fighter!*

Day 120

Determined to Reflect Him

Then God said, "Let Us make man like Us and let him be head over the fish of the sea, and over the birds of the air, and over the cattle, and over all the earth, and over every thing that moves on the ground." And God made man in His own likeness. In the likeness of God He made him. He made both male and female.
Genesis 1:26–27

You are made in the likeness of God. That doesn't mean you have His powers. You don't look like God since He has no body. But being made in His image means we have the ability to reflect His character in how we love others.

Are you kind and full of patience for your friends and family? Are you quick to forgive and move on? Are you loyal and loving? When you are these things for the people around you, you're reflecting His image. Yes, it can be a huge challenge to be like Him when you are tired, hungry, hurt, sad, or angry. But you can choose to be anyway.

. . . .

God, I'm determined to be more like You every day. Help me to choose to reflect You to others.

When It Feels Like Forever

Rest in the Lord and be willing to wait for Him.
PSALM 37:7

These days it seems like everyone wants everything faster and faster. We want zero wait time in the drive-through or checkout line. We want Wi-Fi fast and powerful. We want to order from Amazon and have our package on our porch in two days or less. And on and on. Have you ever felt like you had to wait forever (and sometimes "forever" was actually only ten minutes!) to get something you wanted or to do something you wanted to do? We all struggle with this in our own ways!

In our world, it's hard to work on having patience, which the Bible says is a fruit of the Holy Spirit working in us. We're supposed to grow the healthy fruit of patience in our lives, but how do we do that in such an impatient world? We need to take deep breaths when we're waiting and try not to get upset but instead remember that waiting can be good for us. We need to pray, asking God to give us patience and to help us trust in His perfect timing!

Dear God, I tend to be so impatient, and the world around me doesn't help me much to overcome that. I need Your help to grow in patience. Remind me what a good thing patience is and all the good ways You might be working during wait times! Amen.

Day 122

Rewrite the Bully Thoughts

We break down every thought and proud thing that puts itself up against the wisdom of God. We take hold of every thought and make it obey Christ.
2 CORINTHIANS 10:5

What are the mean things you think about yourself? Do you think you're too short, too freckly, or not thin enough? Have you decided you lack talent or smarts? Maybe you bully yourself with other unkind thoughts.

Paul's advice in 2 Corinthians is awesome! He's challenging you to take those bad thoughts to God and ask His opinion. God loves every bit of your awesomeness. And while you may struggle to embrace it, He doesn't.

The next time you bully yourself with a mean thought, write it down. Think about when you started to believe it. How and why does that thought exist? Then ask God to tell you what He thinks. Write His thoughts next to your own, and then thank Him for the truth. When you do this, you're taking hold of those bully words and replacing them with God's.

....

God, help me to stand up to the bully thoughts and rewrite them. I want to see me the way You do.

Power to Rescue

*So Peter was held in prison. But the church
kept praying to God for him.*
ACTS 12:5

It's so important to read the whole Word of God and be reminded of and encouraged by the many examples of God's work in response to people's prayers. As the church kept on praying for Peter while he was in prison, God moved to rescue Peter in a miraculous way:

> The night before Herod was to bring him out for his trial, Peter was sleeping between two soldiers. He was tied with two chains. Soldiers stood by the door and watched the prison.
>
> All at once an angel of the Lord was seen standing beside him. A light shone in the building. The angel hit Peter on the side and said, "Get up!" Then the chains fell off his hands. The angel said, "Put on your belt and shoes!" He did. The angel said to Peter, "Put on your coat and follow me." Peter followed him out. He was not sure what was happening as the angel helped him. He thought it was a dream.
>
> They passed one soldier, then another one. They came to the big iron door that leads to the city and it opened by itself and they went through. As soon as they had gone up one street, the angel left him.
>
> Peter said to himself, "Now I am sure the Lord has sent His angel and has taken me out of the hands of Herod. He has taken me also from all the things the Jews wanted to do to me" (Acts 12:6–11).

Dear God, You are powerful!

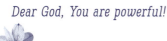

Day 124

Mind Games

You will keep the man in perfect peace whose mind is kept on You, because he trusts in You.
ISAIAH 26:3

Peace comes when you trust God. That may sound easy, but you know giving up control is so hard because it means you don't know how it will all turn out. And honestly, that's kind of scary.

Can you think of a situation you're in right now where you feel restless and fearful? Maybe you're not sleeping well at night or you're cranky with your parents because it feels so heavy. Is it a struggle with a friend or with grades? Something at home or with a teammate? Maybe you're wrestling to make the right choice when the wrong choice feels easier. Regardless, your mind is anything but calm.

Ask God for peace. Spend time in prayer sharing with God what's worrying you. He'll make peace available to you at any moment and in any situation. He'll make those mind games settle down so your heart can rest.

....

God, give me the confidence in You to ask for Your peace rather than try to control everything. Help me trust You more than I trust myself.

Prayer for Your Family

*"Honor your father and your mother, so your life may
be long in the land the Lord your God gives you."*
Exodus 20:12

It's a big job to be a mom or a dad, so I hope you're praying for your parents. Good parents do so much to take good care of you. You're not always going to get along perfectly with them, but God's Word teaches you to honor and obey them. In what ways do you find it hardest and easiest to obey Mom and Dad? Do you need to work on being willing to obey with a good attitude, even when obedience is hard? You encourage and bless your parents when you obey without complaining, and even more importantly, you please God.

You also help your parents and please God when you get along well with your siblings. So pray for good relationships in your whole family. Think of your family as the best kind of team—all of you with different skills to contribute and everyone valuable and needed. If you're usually fighting and upset with each other, you can't really accomplish anything. But a family working together as a team that loves and serves God is unstoppable!

....

*Dear God, I need Your help to do my best to always
honor and obey my parents plus regularly pray for them.
I want our family to be a team that works together well
to bring You glory. That's a real win, for sure! Amen.*

More Prayer for Family

But those who won't care for their relatives, especially those in their own household, have denied the true faith. Such people are worse than unbelievers.
1 TIMOTHY 5:8 NLT

The Bible is clear that we need to look out for one another in our families, not only the ones in our household like our parents and siblings but also our extended family—grandparents, aunts, uncles, and cousins. As a kid you might wonder what you can do to take care of others in your family, but you can always encourage family members and you can always pray for their needs. At reunions and get-togethers and celebrations, you can make the best of whatever time you spend with your extended family. You can share God's love, and if there is conflict, you can try to help resolve it and be forgiving of others. God placed you in your family. Thank Him for each person and ask Him to help you be a loving member of your family.

Dear God, I love my family, and You love them even more. Please help us to have good relationships. And please help any family members who don't believe in You to ask You to be their Savior. Show me what I can do to share Your truth with them. Amen.

Day 127

Is That a Tomorrow Worry?

"Do not worry about tomorrow. Tomorrow will have its own worries. The troubles we have in a day are enough for one day."
MATTHEW 6:34

What are you worried about right now? Is it a test at school or an art project coming due? Do you have a solo in the choir program, or is your team playing in the championship? Are you moving to a new town or about to have a hard conversation with your parents? There is no shortage of worry opportunities, is there? Sometimes we carry weeks of worry on our shoulders and eventually break down in tears because it's just too much.

But God tells us to stay in today's concerns. It's hard to do, but it will help keep fear from overwhelming you. When a tomorrow worry pops into your mind, boldly say out loud, "That's not for today, so go away." Being proactive like that protects your heart and mind and keeps you focused on the things that need your attention today.

....

God, give me only enough strength to carry today's worries. And remind me to keep tomorrow's worries for tomorrow.

Sending in the Troops

For He will tell His angels to care for you and keep you in all your ways. They will hold you up in their hands. So your foot will not hit against a stone.
Psalm 91:11–12

Do you and your friends stick together when a messy situation comes along? Maybe the mean girl was extra mean to you today, or you found out someone was gossiping about you, and without even asking, your friends showed up to help. They protected your heart from more hurt. They told you truth to combat upsetting lies. They made sure you had support and care as they walked through the messy mess with you. Girlfriends are the best, right?

God has your back too. Without asking, He sends in His heavenly troops on your behalf. His angels have been given assignments to care and keep you. They're a line of protection to keep you safe, and they have saved you from things in life you may never even know about.

Rest assured, you are surrounded by earthly and heavenly support every day.

God, thank You! I can have confidence to take the next right step in any situation I face.

Day 129

Walking in Love

*Live this free life by loving and helping others.
You obey the whole Law when you do this one thing,
"Love your neighbor as you love yourself."*
GALATIANS 5:13–14

Our favorite walks around our neighborhood are at Christmastime, as we look at all the Christmas lights decorating people's houses! It's chilly in Ohio (okay, sometimes freezing actually!) but such a fun and beautiful time. We usually take mugs of hot cocoa with us too. Yum!

An even better type of walk around your neighborhood, at any time of the year, is a prayer walk. Focus your mind on praying for the people who live in each house. God wants you to reach out to other people and share His love, and your neighbors who live close by provide a great opportunity for that! On a prayer walk, you can get some healthy exercise plus ask God to show you opportunities to share His love with the specific people He has placed in your community.

....

Dear God, thank You for my neighborhood and the people in it. You know and love every single person. Please show me how You want me to share Your love with them. Amen.

Hard Work and God's Help

*With Your help I can go against many soldiers.
With my God I can jump over a wall.*
PSALM 18:29

Chances are, you'll never have to fight alone against an army or jump over a towering wall. In today's verse, the psalmist is making a powerful point we don't want to miss.

Think about a situation in your life that feels too big. Is it something at school or at home? Maybe something with your own health or a huge family problem? Find something that feels so overwhelming it would take superhuman strength to get through it. It's circumstances like that where we'll only survive with God's help.

He didn't create you to go it alone. Instead, He knew all along that you'd face huge struggles that required more than you had in you. And God also planned all along to be the one to give you the courage and confidence you would need to get through them. Courageous girl, there is nothing you cannot do with hard work and God's help.

....

*God, give me the courage to ask for Your help.
Thanks for always being there for me!*

Day 131

Prayer for Your Church

Those who believed what Peter said were baptized and added to the church that day—about 3,000 in all. All the believers devoted themselves to the apostles' teaching, and to fellowship, and to sharing in meals (including the Lord's Supper), and to prayer.
ACTS 2:41-42 NLT

God's church isn't just a building—it's all believers everywhere! But if you belong to a local church, the people who go there are *your* church family. They all need your prayer. Every time you walk in the doors of your church, you can pray for the protection of your church and the people who come. You can pray for the pastor and leaders and teachers and employees and volunteers of your church. You can pray for the people who are members and the people who attend. You can pray for your church to preach and follow God's Word and glorify Him in everything. You can pray God brings more and more people to hear His truth and experience His love at your church. You can pray to ask God to show you how you can be an active part of your church.

....

Dear God, I pray for my church, my church family, and all those who need to come to my church to learn more about You. I pray that You help me to serve and be active in my church all my life. Amen.

Day 132

You Get to Choose

Do not act like the sinful people of the world. Let God change your life. First of all, let Him give you a new mind. Then you will know what God wants you to do. And the things you do will be good and pleasing and perfect.
ROMANS 12:2

You were created to stand out from everyone else. In all the world—past, present, and future—there will be no one else just like you. God thought you up, every detail. He chose your body type and your skin and hair color. He decided when you'd enter the world and handpicked gifts and talents just for you. To top it off, God gave you a wonderful mind and the ability to think for yourself.

    That means you don't have to follow the crowd. You don't have to think and act like others. Instead, you can be courageous and make the right choices and the hard decisions that glorify God. You have the ability to be strong-minded! Be who God made you to be!

God, renew my mind so I can think for myself and make the best choices in life!

Day 133

Proud Praise

*If anyone wants to be proud, he should be
proud of what the Lord has done.*
2 CORINTHIANS 10:17

Our world talks a lot about being proud of yourself, but the Bible teaches we should be proud of God! He is the one who does all good things and gives us the ability to do good things.

Read what Psalm 34:1–8 says and strive to make it true in your own life:

> I will honor the Lord at all times. His praise will always be in my mouth. My soul will be proud to tell about the Lord. Let those who suffer hear it and be filled with joy. Give great honor to the Lord with me. Let us praise His name together. I looked for the Lord, and He answered me. And He took away all my fears. They looked to Him and their faces shined with joy. Their faces will never be ashamed. This poor man cried, and the Lord heard him. And He saved him out of all his troubles. The angel of the Lord stays close around those who fear Him, and He takes them out of trouble. O taste and see that the Lord is good. How happy is the man who trusts in Him!

God, I want to be proud of You alone. Help me to see how every good thing I ever do ultimately comes from You! Amen.

The Reason You Don't Give Up

This is the reason we do not give up. Our human body is wearing out. But our spirits are getting stronger every day.
2 CORINTHIANS 4:16

Wanting to give up is part of being human. When things get really hard, it's normal to want to quit. We lose heart because we get tired of our situation. Don't feel you're bad or wrong when these feelings come. Instead, decide that today's pain and frustration won't win.

When you feel weakest is when God's strength in you is the brightest! You can ask Him for tools to keep the faith alive and to help you stay focused. Know this: You don't have to give in to peer pressure. You don't have to walk away from friendships that are tough. You don't have to give up on your dreams. You don't have to do what everyone else does just to fit in. When those moments of weakness come, all you have to do is choose to stand strong and ask God for help.

....

God, strengthen me! I need You to fill me with boldness so I can get through whatever comes my way.

Day 135

Mary's Praise

The angel said to her, "Mary, do not be afraid. You have found favor with God. See! You are to become a mother and have a Son. You are to give Him the name Jesus."
LUKE 1:30-31

Mary was just an ordinary girl, chosen to serve God in an extraordinary way—by being the mother of the Savior of the world, Jesus! When Mary learned this, at first she was in shock and had some serious questions for the angel sent to tell her the news. But once her questions were answered, she said, "I am willing to be used of the Lord. Let it happen to me as you have said" (Luke 1:38). And when she shared the news with her cousin Elizabeth, she said:

> "My heart sings with thanks for my Lord. And my spirit is happy in God, the One Who saves from the punishment of sin. The Lord has looked on me, His servant-girl and one who is not important. But from now on all people will honor me. He Who is powerful has done great things for me. His name is holy. The loving-kindness of the Lord is given to the people of all times who honor Him." (Luke 1:46-50)

We can be like Mary, willing to serve God in any way, even ways that seem impossible at first, and ready to praise Him for His awesome works through His people!

Dear God, help me to be willing, like Mary, to serve You in any way You ask. I praise You and honor You! Amen.

Day 136

It All Works Together

We know that God makes all things work together for the good of those who love Him and are chosen to be a part of His plan.
ROMANS 8:28

What a great truth. Somehow, in God's awesomeness, He takes everything you're dealing with and makes it good. That means all the hurt and pain. . .all the sadness and tears. . .all the frustration and anger—they're not wasted. He takes them all and creates something wonderful—something that benefits you.

Maybe you and your bestie had a bad fight, and when you finally worked it out, your friendship got stronger. Maybe your parents grounded you, and spending time at home made you realize how much you enjoyed hanging out with them. Or maybe you got a bad grade on a test, making you work even harder, and you ended up with an awesome grade in the class!

Next time something hard happens, fearlessly trust that God is working on your behalf to make something beautiful out of it. As a matter of fact, thank Him in advance!

....

God, I choose to trust that You will make good from the bad and happy from the sad!

Day 137

When We Need to Slow Down

You must all be quick to listen, slow to speak, and slow to get angry.
JAMES 1:19 NLT

Sometimes we need a whole lot of prayer to obey what the Bible says about anger. It's just so easy to feel angry and let it quickly overtake us. Anger is not always bad; in fact, sometimes it's quite good. It can help protect us and protect others. Like if a bully were to hit you or someone else, of course you should be mad and try to protect yourself or others so the bully cannot hurt someone again. And Jesus became very angry at times (John 2:13–17), and He is the only perfect human being!

But other times we just get mad and let our emotions take over when what we actually need is to slow down, take a deep breath, and figure out *why* we're feeling so mad. It's not bad to feel anger; it's what we do with it that matters. We need to control it and deal with it in healthy ways and not hurt others with angry words or actions. And if we do hurt others, we need to apologize and ask forgiveness and make things right. Be sure to ask a trusted grown-up for help if you feel like you have lots of anger and don't know what to do with it.

....

Dear God, sometimes I feel too angry too quickly over things that shouldn't upset me so much. Will You help me to slow down in these times? I don't want to hurt others with angry words or actions. Will You show me a person who would best be able to talk this out with me? Thank You for knowing all my emotions and for loving and caring for me! Amen.

Day 138

Who Gets the Credit?

It is God Who covers me with strength and makes my way perfect.
PSALM 18:32

Sometimes we think we're all that, taking credit when things go right. We decide we are the reason the team won or the problem was solved. Other times we give the rock star celebrity status to someone else, sure they're why things worked out. But the truth is that God is the one who we should be thanking.

While liking yourself and knowing your talents and skills is good and important, it's also valuable to remember that your courage, strength, and smarts come from God. Whether you realize it or not, He plays a role in your everyday life, helping you out when you need it. God covers you and directs you.

Take time today thanking God for the ways He has helped you. Ask Him for the eyes to see Him working in your life. And the next time you're able to be brave, brilliant, or bold, let God know you're thankful for Him!

....

God, I give You the credit! Thank You for helping me live the right life!

Day 139

Unified Teamwork

"May they experience such perfect unity that the world will know that you sent me and that you love them as much as you love me."
JOHN 17:23 NLT

In our family, we're not big into video games, but we do like to play some family fun ones together. Recently we tried a new one called *Overcooked*. It's a fun, silly game where we need to practice good teamwork to make the right food in time to fulfill the customers' orders.

Good teamwork is necessary in a lot of areas of life. You've probably experienced this in sports or group projects at school. Did you know Jesus specifically prayed for good teamwork among Christians? He prayed for unity, that all of His followers through all of time would be like one team together with God the Father and Jesus the Son, working together to share God's love and help more and more people believe in Jesus. Here is Jesus' prayer in John 17:20–21, 23 (NLT):

> "I am praying not only for these disciples but also for all who will ever believe in me through their message. I pray that they will all be one, just as you and I are one—as you are in me, Father, and I am in you. And may they be in us so that the world will believe you sent me. . . . May they experience such perfect unity that the world will know that you sent me and that you love them as much as you love me."

Dear God, help me to do my part well and promote unity among Jesus followers so that we can win at sharing Your love and helping others know Jesus as Savior. Amen.

Day 140

We All Need Help

"See, God saves me. I will trust and not be afraid. For the Lord God is my strength and song. And He has become the One Who saves me."
ISAIAH 12:2

Can you think of a situation in your life right now where you need God's help? Something that worries you and stresses you out. Something that keeps you awake at night and is all you can think about during the day.

It could be a sick parent or grandparent or another family member who is making bad choices. It may be teammates who aren't getting along, and you're caught in the middle trying to fix it. It could even be a nasty rumor going around school about you that is hurtful and untrue. We all have those situations that feel too big.

Why not talk to God about them? He is trustworthy and faithful, and He promises to save you when things are overwhelming and life feels out of control. Your job is to trust Him and ask for what you need.

....

God, I cannot do this by myself anymore. Will You give me the courage and strength to do what needs to be done?

Day 141

Prayer for Protectors

"No one can have greater love than to give his life for his friends."
JOHN 15:13

Do you have any family members or friends who serve in the military or on a police force? They are our protectors of safety and freedom, and we should be so grateful for them. You can think of ways to honor and encourage them—things like taking treats to share with your local police station, sending cards and packages to service members who are overseas, and always thanking a person in military uniform for their service. Most importantly, you can pray for their safety as they work to keep others safe and free. Especially pray that all of them will know Jesus as their Savior!

Dear God, those who work in the armed forces and police forces are so brave and give so much to others, knowing their life could be taken at any time as they work to protect others' lives. Please bless and help and protect them in extraspecial ways. Amen.

Day 142

Choosing the Right Thing

Jesus said to her, "Martha, Martha, you are worried and troubled about many things. Only a few things are important, even just one. Mary has chosen the good thing. It will not be taken away from her."
LUKE 10:41–42

Martha and Mary were sisters. When Jesus came to their house for a visit, Martha got frustrated that her younger sister sat with the Lord rather than help in the kitchen. She was so angry, in fact, that she went to Jesus and complained, asking Him to tell Mary she needed to get back to work. Today's verse is His response to Martha's request.

What would you have done if Jesus was sitting in your house? Would you have wanted to make pizza rolls in the kitchen or sit with Him as He talked? Every day you get to choose if you spend time with God or if you don't. There are tons of other things that demand our attention. Are you determined enough to choose the right thing?

....

God, I want to make time for You every day. Give me the strength to choose You over other things.

Day 143

Follow the Leader

"The Holy Spirit is coming. He will lead you into all truth. He will not speak His Own words. He will speak what He hears. He will tell you of things to come. He will honor Me. He will receive what is Mine and will tell it to you. Everything the Father has is Mine. That is why I said to you, 'He will receive what is Mine and will tell it to you.'"
JOHN 16:13–15

Do you ever wish you had special powers like you see in your favorite superhero movie? Sometimes I think I need a superpower allowing me to see into the future, warning me of danger and bad situations. And then I remember that in a way, all of us who have the Holy Spirit because we believe in Jesus (Romans 8) *do* have that superpower. We can pray like this. . .

Dear God, I can't see into the future, but I know You can. I need Your Holy Spirit in me to warn me of danger and situations that would be bad for me. Please raise red flags and lead me away from what is harmful for me. Point me toward what is good for me, according to Your will. I don't need to be worried or afraid of the future; I simply need to trust and depend on You, Your power, Your perfect plans, and Your love. Amen.

Day 144

God Knows What's Best

Be happy in the Lord. And He will give you the desires of your heart.
PSALM 37:4

This can be a tricky verse to understand. Some may think it means that whatever you want—cool clothes, a new iPhone, popularity—will be given to you because God wants you happy. Wouldn't that be awesome if it was that easy?

Instead, this verse is saying God will give you the desires of your heart *if* they align with His will for you. And if you are happy in the Lord, it's because you choose to trust His plan for your life. He knows what you want, and at the same time He knows what is best for you. Sometimes those two line up, and sometimes they don't. But regardless, you can be happy because you know God will take care of you either way.

Walking this out takes courage because it's choosing to be okay with God's plan even if it goes against what you really want. Sometimes it's hard to give up what you think is best.

....

God, I want to be happy in You! Help me to trust that Your way is the best way for me.

Day 145

Show Others How to Live

*Let no one show little respect for you because you are young.
Show other Christians how to live by your life. They should
be able to follow you in the way you talk and in what you do.
Show them how to live in faith and in love and in holy living.*
1 TIMOTHY 4:12

You might be young, but that never means that what you do doesn't matter. You can ask God right now to help you make your life an example to others showing how to follow Jesus and live in faith and love and goodness. How can you do that? By respecting and obeying Mom and Dad and helping out at home. By working to get along well with siblings. By showing kindness and love in everything you do. By being generous to others and helping take care of the needy. By doing your best at your schoolwork and in your activities. By admitting mistakes and asking forgiveness. By loving God with everything in you and loving others as yourself. By sharing with others that Jesus is your Savior and He wants to be theirs too. And by following 1 Corinthians 10:31: "Whatever you do, do everything to honor God."

. . . .

*Dear God, help me to remember that the way I live
my life at every age matters. I want to honor You
in everything and be an example to others of what
it means to truly love and obey You. Amen.*

Jesus Is the One

Let us keep looking to Jesus. Our faith comes from Him and He is the One Who makes it perfect. He did not give up when He had to suffer shame and die on a cross. He knew of the joy that would be His later. Now He is sitting at the right side of God.
HEBREWS 12:2

The only one who can truly strengthen your faith is Jesus. Of course, there are some pretty awesome people and places that help point you to Him, like friends, youth group, church, and family. There are also circumstances you have to face that force you to hold on to Jesus. No doubt, God gives you many opportunities to grow your faith and relationship in Jesus.

But we get into trouble when we let anyone or anything take the place of Jesus. Your bestie is the bestest, but she is not better than Jesus. Your mom is magnificent, but she can't out-magnify Him. And youth group is great, but Jesus is greater.

Be grateful for those gifts, but let God give you strength and courage.

God, You are my everything! Grow my faith to perfection!

Day 147

Keep Growing

And this is my prayer: I pray that your love will grow more and more.
PHILIPPIANS 1:9

This prayer from Paul for the Philippians continues, "I pray that you will have better understanding and be wise in all things. I pray that you will know what is the very best. I pray that you will be true and without blame until the day Christ comes again. And I pray that you will be filled with the fruits of right living. These come from Jesus Christ, with honor and thanks to God" (Philippians 1:9–11).

We can study and copy this prayer because it applies to all believers of Jesus. And all believers can pray it for each other too. Healthy, true Christians won't ever want to stop growing in love and in understanding of God and His Word.

. . . .

Dear God, like Paul prayed, I want to have love that grows more and more; I want to have better understanding and be wise in all things; I want to know what is best; I want to be true and blameless; I want to be filled with the fruits that come from living right. I know all good things come from You, and I praise You! Amen.

Day 148

He Holds Your Hand

"For I am the Lord your God Who holds your right hand, and Who says to you, 'Do not be afraid. I will help you.'"
ISAIAH 41:13

God is right here with you, right now. You may not be able to see Him with your eyes or feel Him holding your hand, but chances are you can remember ways He's been there for you.

Think back over the past week. Where have you seen God move? Did He restore a friendship or give you supernatural memory during a test? Did He give you a big dose of hope when things looked hopeless? Did God comfort you in your sadness or give you courage to take the next step? God promises to help whenever you need it.

When you start to feel afraid or overwhelmed, stop and pray for His help. Don't let time pass, because that's when worry starts to pile up. He is ready and waiting to take your hand and lead you to the answers you need.

. . . .

God, I know You've been working in my life even though I can't see Your face or feel Your touch. Help me to live fearlessly, trusting You!

Day 149

All Kinds of Tests

Dear friends, your faith is going to be tested as if it were going through fire. Do not be surprised at this.
1 PETER 4:12

Tests at school aren't just the kind with paper and pencil or on the computer. Of course there are those, but you also have tests of your faith at school. There will always be difficult challenges and people to deal with, and you'll be tested in how you handle these situations. Will you pray and let God help in each and every one? Will you do your best and be a good team player when working on group projects? Will you avoid peer pressure to do things you know are wrong? Will you reach out in kindness to the classmate others are picking on? All of these are opportunities to prove your faith and grow your faith.

During these tests, the Bible says you are to "be happy that you are able to share some of the suffering of Christ. When His shining-greatness is shown, you will be filled with much joy. If men speak bad of you because you are a Christian, you will be happy because the Spirit of shining-greatness and of God is in you" (1 Peter 4:13–14).

....

Dear God, help me to see every kind of test as a chance to prove and show my faith in You. I ask You to help me in all things, and I know You will! Amen.

Fear from the Unexpected

The angel said to the women, "Do not be afraid. I know you are looking for Jesus Who was nailed to the cross. He is not here! He has risen from the dead as He said He would. Come and see the place where the Lord lay. Run fast and tell His followers that He is risen from the dead. He is going before you to the country of Galilee. You will see Him there as I have told you."
MATTHEW 28:5-7

Maybe you can relate to the woman in today's scripture. She expected one thing, but something totally different happened instead. And in that confusing moment, she was scared!

Can you relate to her instant fear? The unexpected can be scary because we're not sure what to do next. Like when you thought you rocked the test, but the failing grade is staring back at you. Or when you find a seat next to your friend at lunch, and she ignores you. We get confused, and that confusion turns to fear. But fear is never from God. And He will replace it with courage.

....

God, help me to stay brave when the unexpected hits.

Like a Lion

Keep awake! Watch at all times. The devil is working against you. He is walking around like a hungry lion with his mouth open. He is looking for someone to eat. Stand against him and be strong in your faith.
1 PETER 5:8–9

The Lincoln Park Zoo in Chicago is a very cool zoo to visit. I was there once in college with a friend, and when we stopped to see the lion, we got quite the close-up view of him. He was walking right near the front of his enclosure, so if not for the glass, we easily could have touched him. As we watched him, he suddenly let out a powerful roar! It was amazing to hear that sound so close to us, and definitely a little scary too! I can't imagine meeting up with a lion like that out in the wild—yikes!

I need to picture that lion and remember that fear as I remind myself of 1 Peter 5:8–9. We all do. We have an enemy, the devil, who is like a hungry lion lurking around with his mouth open, ready to destroy us. The only way to stand strong against him is to stand strong in our faith.

Dear God, keep me steadfast in believing in and obeying You so I can stand strong against the enemy who wants to destroy me. Amen.

Day 152

Oh Yes, You Are Loved!

"The Lord your God is with you, a Powerful One Who wins the battle. He will have much joy over you. With His love He will give you new life. He will have joy over you with loud singing."
ZEPHANIAH 3:17

Ever feel unloved, like you're just a piece of trash blowing in the wind? The truth is that every day, plenty of things happen to make you feel worthless. Maybe your friend got mad at you, your parents are disappointed in you, or your coach is frustrated at your performance. So what do you do when it seems like everyone dislikes you?

Try asking God what He thinks. He sees the truth about you and knows how amazing you are because He thought you up. Even more, God so delights in you that He literally sings over you! Even with your mess-ups, you bring Him great joy! And there is nothing you can do to make God love you any more or less than He does right now. Oh yes, courageous girl. You are very loved, indeed.

. . . .

*God, thank You for loving me so much!
I'm glad nothing I do will change that!*

Tears in a Bottle

You keep track of all my sorrows. You have collected all my tears in your bottle. You have recorded each one in your book.
PSALM 56:8 NLT

It's awful that it's true, but our hearts get broken a lot in this world, over lots of different kinds of things. God never intended our world to be full of sadness and sickness and death and pain, but when sin entered the world, so did all those bad things. Through each difficult circumstance that makes us cry, we must always believe how much God cares about each of our sorrows. The Bible promises He is near when we are brokenhearted. He heals us (Psalm 34:18; 147:3); He knows and cares about every single one of our sad tears (Psalm 56:8); and for all who believe in Jesus, He is preparing heaven, where "He will wipe every tear from their eyes, and there will be no more death or sorrow or crying or pain. All these things are gone forever" (Revelation 21:4 NLT).

When you are hurting, pray to God and cry to Him. Let Him collect your tears. Focus on the truth of these scriptures. He will help you keep going and keep finding joy, and one day He will make everything right.

....

Dear God, please help me when I am heartbroken. I need Your comfort and I need to remember the truth of Your Word. Thank You for caring about every tear I cry. I trust You and want to follow You no matter what. Amen.

Day 154

"Even If" Kind of Faith

Even if the fig tree does not grow figs and there is no fruit on the vines, even if the olives do not grow and the fields give no food, even if there are no sheep within the fence and no cattle in the cattle-building, yet I will have joy in the Lord. I will be glad in the God Who saves me.
HABAKKUK 3:17–18

This is a beautiful truth. The author of these verses is showing what fearless faith looks like. No matter what's happened, the writer knows God is still good. He knows God is still able. And that's the kind of faith we all need.

"Even if" kind of faith says no matter the yucky and hard circumstances you're facing today, you can still have joy because of Jesus. Your family could be having a tough time, your best friends may turn against you, or you could've been cut from the school play. . .but these things don't take away your ability to smile. Why? Because your joy comes from God rather than from anything the world offers.

God, give me the grit I need to have "even if" kind of faith!

Pray for Fruit

But the Holy Spirit produces this kind of fruit in our lives: love, joy, peace, patience, kindness, goodness, faithfulness, gentleness, and self-control. There is no law against these things!
GALATIANS 5:22–23 NLT

If you search Google, you can find some really fun songs about the fruits of the Spirit to help you remember them. As you learn and sing those songs, make these fruits part of your regular prayers. Ask God to grow them abundantly in your life and to help you share them with others.

And if you write in a prayer journal, keep track of how you see God growing the fruits of the Spirit in your life and whom He has asked you to share them with. You might write something like, *I really needed extra gentleness with my little sister today, and I prayed and God gave it.* Or *I felt like I would have zero self-control over my words when a classmate made me mad today, but I prayed and God helped me choose my words carefully.*

If you keep a record, you can look back later and remember and thank God and let your faith be made even stronger!

. . . .

Dear God, I want to see more love, joy, peace, patience, kindness, goodness, faithfulness, gentleness, and self-control in my life. Please let Your Holy Spirit grow these in my life so I can share them with others. Amen.

No Drama Llama

*Let the peace of Christ have power over your hearts.
You were chosen as a part of His body. Always be thankful.*
COLOSSIANS 3:15

Would your family and friends say you're a drama llama? If they were to be completely honest, do you think they'd say you tend to exaggerate your feelings? Or would they say you're pretty steady no matter what comes your way?

Some of us are naturally a bit more dramatic in how we respond to life's heartaches and fears, but let's not forget that we also have the gift of choice. We can choose to overreact, or we can choose to take a deep breath and stay calm. No matter our usual, our responses can change if we ask God for help. When we do, He can tame the drama-llama-ness so we can live with a peaceful heart.

So the next time you get scared or hurt. . .the next time you fail or give up. . .the next time you want to freak out. . .be bold enough to ask for the peace of Christ instead.

*God, thank You for making Your peace
available to me whenever and wherever!*

No Potatoes!

Do you not know that your body is a house of God where the Holy Spirit lives? God gave you His Holy Spirit. Now you belong to God. You do not belong to yourselves. God bought you with a great price. So honor God with your body. You belong to Him.
1 CORINTHIANS 6:19–20

What are your favorite ways to get healthy exercise for your body? Jodi and Lilly love to jump on our trampoline (especially when it's raining!), swim, and dance. There are so many fun ways for kids to stay active and healthy. And so many options for healthy foods too!

Sadly, there are a whole lot of ways to grow unhealthy too. Watching too much television, playing too many video games, and eating too much junk food, to name just a few. These things are fine to enjoy here and there, but too much and they can turn you into a couch potato with major health problems later on.

Start praying now, and continue your whole life, to see your body the way God sees it: dearly loved and a place where His Holy Spirit lives! He wants you to take good care of this home for the Holy Spirit so that while you're here on earth, you can do the wonderful things He has planned for you to do to share His love.

Dear God, I need Your help to want to stay active and healthy my whole life. The world has a lot of ways to tempt me to become a couch potato, and I don't want that. Amen.

Every Single One

Give all your worries to Him because He cares for you.
1 PETER 5:7

Reread today's verse out loud. Just how many of your worries does God want you to give to Him? One a day? Ten a week? Just the important ones? No, courageous girl. God wants every single one of your worries—the big, the small, and everything in between.

Why? Because He loves you so much and He knows life gets hard, scary, and overwhelming. He didn't create you to carry everything alone. You simply aren't that strong or powerful. In His unstoppable love for you, He chose to be available and willing to help you carry those things that feel too big and too hard.

Take a minute to let all your worries come to mind right now. For each one, tell God your fears surrounding each worry and then imagine handing them over to Him. See yourself holding the worry and then watch what happens as you place it in His hands.

....

God, I give You all my worries because I cannot hold them anymore. Thank You for taking them from me!

Day 159

No Matter What

*Heal me, O Lord, and I will be healed.
Save me and I will be saved. For You are my praise.*
JEREMIAH 17:14

Sometimes no matter how hard you try to stay healthy and take care of your body, sickness or injury comes your way anyway. That totally stinks! Minor colds and such are no big deal, but maybe you've dealt or are dealing with a much scarier illness or injury. If not you, surely you know someone who is, and that person needs extra special prayer!

Anyone struggling with illness or injury should learn about the life and faith of Joni Eareckson Tada. Actually, every healthy person should too. She's amazing! I encourage you to read her books and watch her movie and listen to her on the radio or through her website. Her arms and legs were paralyzed in a diving accident at just seventeen years old. Her body that was once young and healthy and able to do so many fun activities was suddenly able to do almost nothing without help. Joni had to work through so much sadness and anger and pain to learn to cope with her lifelong condition of being paralyzed. And she is one of the greatest leaders of faith in our world today, proving again and again for over fifty years in all kinds of physical hardship that she trusts God and sees Him at work in her life through her condition. She has helped countless other people with their injuries and illnesses too.

. . . .

Dear God, thank You. You help with the pain and struggle; You heal according to Your will; and You give us amazing opportunities to grow our faith in You. Amen.

Day 160

Are You Asking?

*"Until now you have not asked for anything in My name.
Ask and you will receive. Then your joy will be full."*
JOHN 16:24

As Jesus girls, we're invited to ask God for what we need. Sometimes we think it's silly to ask for the small stuff, but God doesn't. We may think He is too busy to find time to listen as we ask for help with an upcoming test or frustrating friendships. We may think sharing concerns about our health or our family or even the upcoming tryouts is wasting His time. But that is absolutely not how God feels.

What keeps you from asking Him for help? You are free to ask for anything you need. God wants to have a relationship with you. And just like you have the freedom to ask your friends, your parents, your teachers, or your youth leaders for the things you need, you have that same open-door policy with God.

*God, help me to be bold enough to ask You for help.
Remind me that You are able and willing to
meet every need I have.*

Day 161

No Grumpy Givers!

Remember this—a farmer who plants only a few seeds will get a small crop. But the one who plants generously will get a generous crop. You must each decide in your heart how much to give. And don't give reluctantly or in response to pressure. "For God loves a person who gives cheerfully." And God will generously provide all you need. Then you will always have everything you need and plenty left over to share with others.
2 Corinthians 9:6–8 nlt

Do you have favorite toys and collections that you can't imagine ever giving up? We all like to love our favorite stuff. But we have to be very careful with this. We should never love any certain things more than we love God and want to obey Him. And that requires a lot of prayer!

Start praying now to love being a giver much more than being a getter. Pray to be a sharer rather than a hoarder. And ask God to help you always be happy to give. His Word says He wants us to be cheerful givers, not grumpy ones who only give because we're forced to because we're afraid we'll get in trouble if we don't.

....

Dear God, I need Your help all the time to love being a giver much more than I love being a getter. Please grow joy and cheer in me over being generous and sharing with others. I want to remember that every good thing ultimately comes from You! Amen.

Day 162

The Boldness of Prayer

Never stop praying.
1 THESSALONIANS 5:17

The Bible tells us to pray about everything. But what is prayer, and how do we do it?

Prayer is how you talk to your heavenly Father. You can talk out loud to Him, or you can pray silently. You can have long or short prayers. They don't have to sound proper or intelligent. You can even pray using bad grammar or run-on sentences.

There isn't a right time or a wrong time to pray. There's no limit on the number of prayers you can send God's way or the things you can pray about. You don't have to follow rules or guidelines. And yes, you can be bold in what you ask God to do. He wants to hear it all. You can pray directly to God anywhere, at any time, about anything.

So whether it's about something that scares you or someone who's hurt you. . .pray. If it's excitement over getting the lead in a play. . .pray. If you need to share a secret or vent in anger. . .pray. God is always listening.

God, give me confidence to talk to You about everything!

Day 163

Hezekiah's Prayer

"Now, O Lord our God, I beg You to save us."
2 KINGS 19:19

Even if you never become a leader of a nation, like Hezekiah was king of Judah, you can be inspired by how he prayed when all the cities of Judah were captured by enemies and everything seemed hopeless:

> Hezekiah prayed to the Lord, saying, "O Lord the God of Israel, You sit on Your throne above the cherubim. You are the God, and You alone, of all the nations of the earth. You have made heaven and earth. Turn Your ear, O Lord, and hear. Open Your eyes, O Lord, and see. Listen to the words Sennacherib has spoken against the living God. O Lord, it is true that the kings of Assyria have destroyed the nations and their lands. They have thrown their gods into the fire. For they were not gods, but the work of men's hands, made from wood and stone. So they have destroyed them. Now, O Lord our God, I beg You to save us from his power. Then all the nations of the earth may know that You alone are God, O Lord." (2 Kings 19:15–19)

God answered Hezekiah's prayer and rescued Judah from the evil Assyrians. (Read on in 2 Kings 19 to find out more.) Let Hezekiah's prayer inspire you to pray like this. . .

. . . .

Dear God, when everything seems hopeless for me and I feel like I have enemies controlling me, please come to my rescue like You did for Hezekiah. I know You can! Amen.

Day 164

The Power of Praying for Others

I pray that because of the riches of His shining-greatness, He will make you strong with power in your hearts through the Holy Spirit. I pray that Christ may live in your hearts by faith. I pray that you will be filled with love. I pray that you will be able to understand how wide and how long and how high and how deep His love is. I pray that you will know the love of Christ. His love goes beyond anything we can understand. I pray that you will be filled with God Himself.
EPHESIANS 3:16–19

In today's passage of scripture, Paul is praying for the church in Ephesus. He knows it's one of the kindest things he can do for the people there, because God listens when we pray.

Do you pray for others? Think of someone who is having a hard time right now. Reread Ephesians 3:16–19, this time using the person's name every time you see the words *you* and *your*. Pray this for anyone God brings to mind. It's how we love others well.

. . . .

God, give me boldness to pray for others.

Day 165

Watch Out for the Waxy Ones

When we obey God, we are sure we know him. But if we claim to know him and don't obey him, we are lying and the truth isn't in our hearts. We truly love God only when we obey him as we should, and then we know that we belong to him. If we say we are his, we must follow the example of Christ.
1 JOHN 2:3–6 CEV

If you've ever gone to a wax museum, you've seen how much something that is fake can look like the real deal. It's amazing how lifelike those wax statues can be! The Bible talks about hypocritical people who say they know Jesus but actually are not real-deal followers of Him. As you get to know and observe them, you find they don't want to obey the Bible and live like Jesus did. We need to pray and be on the lookout for these people and not let them influence us or our faith. And it's so important to keep reading and studying God's Word so we can constantly compare what we are learning with how people are living—especially how we ourselves are living. If we say we know and love Jesus, we should want to be known as real-deal followers of Him, never waxy fake ones!

Dear God, help me to obey You and live like Jesus did. I want to be known for truly loving and living for You. Amen.

Day 166

The Secret Things of God

"The secret things belong to the Lord our God. But the things that are made known belong to us and to our children forever, so we may obey all the words of this Law."
Deuteronomy 29:29

When bad things happen, one of the first questions we ask is *why*. *Why* did this happen to me? *Why* did this happen again? *Why* can't I catch a break? *Why* doesn't God protect me? *Why* can't I get it right? *Why* are they so mean?

What *why* questions do you ask when bad happens in your life?

While it's normal to want answers, the truth is we don't always get to know them here on earth. Actually, we may never understand why we're called to be brave when certain things happen. We have to trust that the things God chooses to keep secret are for a good reason, and if we needed to know the *why*, we would.

The next time *why* questions flood your mind, find courage to let them know you trust God and His decision to keep certain things secret.

God, may my why questions never make me doubt You!

Pray in Line

We thank God for you all the time and pray for you.
1 THESSALONIANS 1:2

Do you spend a lot of time waiting in line? At school and in the cafeteria and at the bus stop? In the checkout aisle at the store with Mom and Dad? Or while you're running errands with them to the bank or post office? I'm not sure I'd ever want to count up all the minutes in my life I've spent waiting in line—I've done a whole lot of it by now. At first it seems like such a waste of time—until you choose to be productive during these moments.

One thing you can always do in lines is use the time to pray! That's never, ever a waste of time! Pray for your own needs and the needs of others, and you can totally pray for the strangers in line with you too; in your mind you can ask God to bless them and help them with whatever their needs and challenges are. Once while I was in line for doughnuts (that's a fun line, for sure!) I felt a strong sense of needing to pray for everyone who was in the doughnut shop with me. I don't know why exactly or how God answered those prayers, but I'm thankful for the chance to be productive in prayer anytime, anywhere!

....

Dear God, please remind me that line time doesn't ever have to be wasted time. You are with me and I can always talk with You about my needs and the needs of others too. Amen.

Which Way Do We Go?

*I will show you and teach you in the way you should go.
I will tell you what to do with My eye upon you.*
Psalm 32:8

With all the choices you'll need to make today, sometimes it's hard to know the right thing to do. It's confusing to make decisions when you're not sure what's best. When you're struggling to choose, who do you ask for help? Who is the person you listen to the most?

We all need friends and family to share their ideas, suggestions, and thoughts when we're looking for answers. They are a gift from God because they love us enough to help us figure out life. But if you aren't asking God for His help, you're missing out.

Your heavenly Father promises to give you direction and show you the next right step to take. Even more, He'll give you the courage you need to make decisions without fear. And He will give you confidence to know you are being smart with your choices.

....

God, teach me and show me what's best for me. I trust You!

Don't Just Doodle and Daydream

Obey the Word of God. If you hear only and do not act, you are only fooling yourself. Anyone who hears the Word of God and does not obey is like a man looking at his face in a mirror. After he sees himself and goes away, he forgets what he looks like. But the one who keeps looking into God's perfect Law and does not forget it will do what it says and be happy as he does it. God's Word makes men free.
JAMES 1:22–25

You could go to school every single day for the rest of your life and never learn anything new—if you choose not to focus. You could just doodle on your paper and daydream and be bored and not care one bit about learning the good things you need to know. I think that sounds like a terrible idea and a total waste of time. I hope it does to you too!

The same is true every time you read God's Word and go to church. You can choose not to focus and care, but then you're totally wasting your time. How sad, right?

Instead, every time you have the chance, you can pray and ask God to help you focus on His Word, learn from His Word, obey His Word, and be a doer of His Word. Then God will help you live your very best life.

....

Dear God, help me to pay attention every time I have the chance to learn more about You, when I read Your Word and when I'm learning at church and with my family. I want to be Your true follower and a doer of Your Word! Amen.

Day 170

Haters Gonna Hate

"Do not say what is wrong in other people's lives. Then other people will not say what is wrong in your life. Do not say someone is guilty. Then other people will not say you are guilty. Forgive other people and other people will forgive you."
LUKE 6:37

Luke 6:37 gives the perfect reason why we should not be haters. It can be hard, because girls are sometimes gossipy and judgy, but that doesn't mean you have to be. And when you are rude about others or talk behind someone's back, it sets you up for the same to happen to you.

But that reality is true on the other side as well. You see, kindness breeds kindness. Be nice to others and they will be nice to you. Forgive others and you'll be forgiven by them too. Love those around you and you will be loved right back.

Don't judge people. Don't be critical. Instead, find the guts and grit to be different. Haters gonna hate, but you can love.

....

God, I don't want to be mean and rude. I know everyone is battling something. Help me to be a force for good in the world.

Don't Be Like a Weed

And now, just as you accepted Christ Jesus as your Lord, you must continue to follow him. Let your roots grow down into him, and let your lives be built on him. Then your faith will grow strong in the truth you were taught, and you will overflow with thankfulness.
COLOSSIANS 2:6–7 NLT

I'm not really a fan of pulling weeds, especially weeds with prickly stems—ouch! Definitely need the gardening gloves for those! One thing I'm always thankful for when pulling weeds is that their roots are shallow and they're usually easy to pull away from the soil they're growing in.

A favorite scripture of mine that I love to pray for Jodi and Lilly (and myself and others too—including you right now as I write this!) is the scripture about roots in Colossians 2:6–7. Asking Jesus to be our Savior is the first wonderful step in a wonderful life of following Him and letting our roots grow into Him and His truth so deeply that nothing can pull us away from Jesus. We don't ever want to be like weeds that can easily be pulled out of our life of following our Savior.

....

Dear God, I sure don't want to be like a weed that can easily be pulled away from real life in You. Help me to be like the sturdiest, tallest tree with my roots grown strong and deep into You.

Day 172

Put On Jesus

I will have much joy in the Lord. My soul will have joy in my God, for He has clothed me with the clothes of His saving power. He has put around me a coat of what is right and good, as a man at his own wedding wears something special on his head, and as a bride makes herself beautiful with stones of great worth.
ISAIAH 61:10

Every day, you get to choose whether you put on Jesus. You can walk out the door full of love and kindness, or you can walk out with bitterness and unforgiveness. When you find your seat in class, you can be a ray of sunshine in that room or a dark cloud of anger. At practice, you can light up that space with joy or fill it with a bad mood. You get to choose.

Even on the days when you want to stay in bed with the covers over your head, you can ask God for the strength to put on Jesus. With Him, you can love your family, friends, classmates, teammates, and everyone you connect with.

God, help me to wear Jesus every day!

Day 173

More about Roots

"A farmer went out to plant his seed. As he scattered it across his field, some seed fell on a footpath, where it was stepped on, and the birds ate it. Other seed fell among rocks. It began to grow, but the plant soon wilted and died for lack of moisture. Other seed fell among thorns that grew up with it and choked out the tender plants. Still other seed fell on fertile soil. This seed grew and produced a crop that was a hundred times as much as had been planted!"
LUKE 8:5–8 NLT

Jesus told this parable about having good strong roots:

"This is the meaning of the parable: The seed is God's word. The seeds that fell on the footpath represent those who hear the message, only to have the devil come and take it away from their hearts and prevent them from believing and being saved. The seeds on the rocky soil represent those who hear the message and receive it with joy. But since they don't have deep roots, they believe for a while, then they fall away when they face temptation. The seeds that fell among the thorns represent those who hear the message, but all too quickly the message is crowded out by the cares and riches and pleasures of this life. And so they never grow into maturity. And the seeds that fell on the good soil represent honest, good-hearted people who hear God's word, cling to it, and patiently produce a huge harvest." (Luke 8:11–15 NLT)

Dear God, help me to have deep roots in You! Amen.

Day 174

The Book of Answers

Your Word is a lamp to my feet and a light to my path.
PSALM 119:105

Sometimes we just need someone to explain things to us, or we need to find a book that gives us all of life's answers. The world is confusing, and people are even more confusing.

Maybe you struggle to understand your siblings or parents. Maybe boys puzzle you because you can't make sense of the things they do. Maybe you don't always get why your friends are fine one minute and then super moody the next. And maybe there are times you can't figure out why you act the way you do or say the things you say.

Wouldn't it be nice to have a handbook that explains it all?

Every time you pick up the Bible, that's exactly what you have. It's your Holy Handbook, and God has addressed every issue inside it. But to access its wisdom, you'll have to spend time reading it. You'll have to choose to open the Bible every day—and stick with it!

God, give me the strength and discipline to dig into Your Word every day so I can live wisely!

Day 175

Out of Trouble

*I cried to the Lord in my trouble, and He answered
me and put me in a good place.*
PSALM 118:5

Once when we were at the beach, Lilly and Jodi dug a deep hole and then Lilly decided to try to crawl headfirst into it. Soon she got stuck with her legs kicking in the air, and Jodi and I laughed hysterically (which Lilly didn't appreciate!) before we helped pull her out. She wasn't in any real danger, but she did feel like she was headfirst in quite a troublesome situation.

Unfortunately, we may experience much worse problems than just being stuck in a sandy hole. You've probably experienced some. How did God help you out of them? Psalm 118 encourages us that we can always cry out to God in our troubles and that He will help us out of them and into a good place. It goes on to say, "The Lord is with me. I will not be afraid of what man can do to me. The Lord is with me. He is my Helper. I will watch those lose who fight against me. It is better to trust in the Lord than to trust in man. It is better to trust in the Lord than to trust in rulers" (Psalm 118:6–9).

....

*Dear Lord, I trust You more than any person or leader.
I know You are always with me, and I don't need to be
afraid of anyone. When I'm in trouble, please help me to
get out of it and get into a good place. Thank You! Amen.*

Day 176

Believing without Seeing

You have never seen Him but you love Him. You cannot see Him now but you are putting your trust in Him. And you have joy so great that words cannot tell about it. You will get what your faith is looking for, which is to be saved from the punishment of sin.
1 PETER 1:8–9

Faith is believing in what you can't see, but it's hard to believe in someone you can't hang out with. It's hard building trust in someone whose face you don't get to see. And you may struggle to have confidence in someone you can't hug or high-five.

But Peter gives an exciting reason to have faith in God, even though you won't get to see Him with your eyes before you're in heaven. He says that if you have the courage to believe in Him, you'll have crazy amounts of joy on earth and get to live with God forever and ever in heaven. All of that for having the strength to believe without seeing.

....

God, may I have faith to trust You always! And thank You for inviting me to live with You forever in heaven!

Public Prayer

*Remember to pray for all Christians. Pray for me also.
Pray that I might open my mouth without fear.*
EPHESIANS 6:18–19

Just recently on vacation in St. Augustine, Florida, Jodi, Lilly, their dad, and I were praying together right before we ate our yummy seafood. And then a lady at the table next to us came over to thank us for praying. She said it was so encouraging to see us do that in public. We were so blessed and encouraged to be a blessing and encouragement to her!

As Christians in the USA where we are totally free to worship and pray to God in public, we should be doing this all the more. There are Christians all around the world who live in places where it's very dangerous to be a follower of Jesus and read the Bible. Unless we've been there, it's hard to even imagine how awful that must be. They desperately need our prayers, all the time. And all the more, then, because they cannot pray in public, we should be grateful we never have to hide our faith and our prayers. And we should share our faith and our prayers, even if simply by bowing our heads and praying aloud, sincerely and humbly, before a meal in a public place to our one true God and our Savior, Jesus Christ.

Dear God, help me never to be scared to pray to You out loud and read my Bible in any public place, especially in a nation where I am totally free to do so! I pray for Your extra-special closeness and care for those Christians all around the world who are in great danger because they follow You. Protect them and strengthen them, please! Amen.

Day 178

Courageous Love Pays Off

*Live and work without pride. Be gentle and kind.
Do not be hard on others. Let love keep you from
doing that. Work hard to live together as one by the
help of the Holy Spirit. Then there will be peace.*
EPHESIANS 4:2–3

Loving others takes courage because it's so hard to do all the time. When people are nice to us, loving them is easy. It doesn't take much work to care for those who save us seats at lunch, invite us to parties, or treat us kindly. But choosing to love people who are mean or rude is another story.

God wants you to be gentle and kind, giving others grace when they don't deserve it. He is asking you to put on your big-girl pants and do everything you can to get along with others. He wants you to be selfless and own your mistakes rather than blame someone else. And you'll be able to live this way by choosing to love those who are easy to love. . .and also choosing to love those people who can be difficult.

*God, help me to have courageous
love for everyone around me!*

Day 179

Keep Learning from Daniel

*He got down on his knees three times each day,
praying and giving thanks to his God, as he had done before.*
DANIEL 6:10

Daniel in the lions' den is a pretty popular story, and even if we think we know it well, it's good to go back and learn from Daniel again and again. Even though Daniel's enemies, who were extremely jealous of him, convinced the king to write a law that said it was illegal for Daniel to pray to anyone other than the king of their time, King Darius, Daniel continued to pray to the one true God. And as punishment for breaking the law, he was thrown into a den of hungry lions. But because Daniel never stopped praying, he was able to witness an amazing miracle—God shut the mouths of the lions so they didn't harm Daniel!

And even more, the next day King Darius was so astonished by this miracle that he chose to believe in God and announced that all the people of his nation should too! The king decreed, "May you have much peace! I make a law that all those under my rule are to fear and shake before the God of Daniel. For He is the living God and He lives forever. His nation will never be destroyed and His rule will last forever. He saves and brings men out of danger, and shows His great power in heaven and on earth. And He has saved Daniel from the power of the lions" (Daniel 6:25–27).

Dear God, help me to have great courage like Daniel, who never stopped praying to You even when he was in great danger. Please also let me see great miracles happen when I follow You no matter what! Amen.

Day 180

Whose Voice Do You Listen To?

*"When the shepherd walks ahead of them,
they follow him because they know his voice."*
JOHN 10:4

There are a lot of voices in the world today. And sometimes it gets confusing to know the right one to listen to because the messages are conflicting—they say different things.

There are the good ones that encourage you to be yourself and to be confident in who you are. They remind you that you're beautiful no matter what and that there's a powerful God who loves you. But there are also voices that say you must look a certain way, be in the right group at school, live in a certain neighborhood, or do things you know are wrong to be loved and accepted. The problem is that so often the loudest voices are the negatives ones.

Whose voices are you listening to these days? What keeps you from only listening to God's? How can you make sure you know the difference between His voice and the negative ones?

....

God, will You give me the strength to choose Your voice over everyone else's? I only want to listen to You because You always have my back.

Three Super-brave Guys

"There are certain Jews whom you have chosen as leaders over the land of Babylon. Their names are Shadrach, Meshach, and Abed-nego. These men have not listened to you, O king. They do not serve your gods or worship the object of gold which you have set up."
DANIEL 3:12

Another famous story we need to revisit often is the one of Daniel's friends with such interesting names: Shadrach, Meshach, and Abed-nego. Even though they were about to be thrown into a fire so hot no one could even get near it without dying, they totally refused to give up their faith in the one true God to worship a false god. God gave them such courage that they were able to say to King Nebuchadnezzar, "If we are thrown into the fire, our God Whom we serve is able to save us from it. And He will save us from your hand, O king. But even if He does not, we want you to know, O king, that we will not serve your gods or worship the object of gold that you have set up" (Daniel 3:17–18).

"Even if He does not," they said. Don't miss that. It's not that they didn't believe God had the power to save them. But they trusted that God's will is always best, no matter what He decides.

. . . .

Dear God—wow!—Shadrach, Meshach, and Abed-nego were so very brave. Please help me to have trust like they did that even if You choose not to answer my prayer, I will never stop believing in You! You are always good and right! Amen.

Day 182

More about Three Super-brave Guys

The three men were still tied up when they fell into the fire.
DANIEL 3:23

God was about to do something no one could have imagined:

> King Nebuchadnezzar. . .said to his leaders, "Did we not throw three men who were tied up into the fire?" They answered, "That is true, O king." He said, "Look! I see four men loose and walking about in the fire without being hurt! And the fourth one looks like a son of the gods (or the Son of God)!" Then Nebuchadnezzar came near the door where the fire was burning, and said, "Shadrach, Meshach and Abed-nego, servants of the Most High God, come out! Come here!". . . The fire had not hurt the bodies of these three men. . . . They did not even smell like fire. Nebuchadnezzar said, "Praise be to the God of Shadrach, Meshach, and Abed-nego. He has sent His angel and saved His servants who put their trust in Him. . . . So I now make a law that if any people of any nation or language say anything against the God of Shadrach, Meshach and Abed-nego, they will be torn apart and their houses will be laid waste. For there is no other god who is able to save in this way." (Daniel 3:24–29)

Dear God, You are amazing! No one is able to save like You! Amen.

Day 183

Why Worry When You Can Pray?

"Which of you can make yourself a little taller by worrying? If you cannot do that which is so little, why do you worry about other things?"
Luke 12:25–26

Worry does nothing to help you. Not one thing. Worrying about a test doesn't make you do better. Instead, it usually makes your brain stop working. Stressing out about a hard conversation doesn't do anything but make you sick to your stomach. Having anxiety about the report you have to give in front of the class does nothing but make you feel insecure. Worry is not your friend.

Rather than lose sleep over the hard things in your day, what if you prayed? While you're brushing your teeth, putting on shoes, or walking into school, why not tell God what has your stomach in knots? Ask Him to give you confidence and courage, strength and determination, and peace and comfort. Since we have prayer, we don't have to give in to worry.

What are you worried about right now? Take a minute and talk to God about it.

....

God, there are so many reasons I get worried.
Help me to ditch the worry and to trust You instead.

Jesus Has Your Back

And so Jesus is able, now and forever, to save from the punishment of sin all who come to God through Him because He lives forever to pray for them.
HEBREWS 7:25

Jesus always speaks up to God for you. Because you delight Him so much, He chose to step out of heaven and down to earth so He could die on the cross to save you from your sins. This verse says that Jesus lives and acts as a mediator on your behalf, and He prays for you continually. He is for you, He loves you, and He cheers you on!

When you ask, Jesus gives you strength. He gives you courage. He fills you with peace and joy. Jesus will heal you, restore you, untangle you, direct you, and bring peace when you're afraid. You may have lots of people on earth who love you, but no one can love you the way Jesus can.

Whenever you feel lonely or unloved, think back on all the ways Jesus proves your worth. Remember all the ways He acts on your behalf. You are precious to Him!

....

God, thank You for Jesus!

Day 185

Prayer for Those Who Are Wearing Out

This is the reason we do not give up. Our human body is wearing out. But our spirits are getting stronger every day. The little troubles we suffer now for a short time are making us ready for the great things God is going to give us forever.
2 CORINTHIANS 4:16–17

Who are the elderly people in your life? Maybe great-grandparents or great-aunts and great-uncles? Maybe you have family members or friends you visit in a nursing home, or an elderly neighbor. If you spend any time around elderly people, you can't help but see the truth of 2 Corinthians 4:16—human bodies definitely wear out.

So pray and ask God how you can be an extra special blessing to the elderly people in your life. Visit them, help them, chat with them, make cards for them, and encourage them in whatever ways you can. Most importantly, remind them that if they know Jesus as Savior, their spirits are getting stronger every day and the troubles for human bodies on this earth are just for a short time. God is going to give great things in heaven forever!

Dear God, please help me to be a big help and encouragement to the elderly people in my life. Show me what I can do for them and how best to share Your truth and love with them. Amen.

Look to God Instead

"Look to the Lord and ask for His strength. Look to Him all the time."
1 CHRONICLES 16:11

When you're in a hard situation, do you crumble and cry. . .or do you start to pray? When you fail at something, do you get angry and agitated. . .or do you talk to God? When it feels like the world is against you, do you scream and sob. . .or do you drop to your knees and give it to the Lord?

So often, our normal response is to freak out. We run to our besties or our parents, hoping they will fix things for us. Or we hide under the covers with a big bowl of ice cream, trying to fill our belly and wishing it would fill our heart too. We look for anything on earth that will make us feel better. But why don't we find the grit to look to God instead?

Courageous girl, God is for you! Bravely let Him know what you need, because He promises to help.

. . . .

God, You are so awesome. I want to look to You for anything and everything.

Day 187

Winds and Waves

Jesus got into a boat. His followers followed Him. At once a bad storm came over the lake. The waves were covering the boat. Jesus was sleeping. His followers went to Him and called, "Help us, Lord, or we will die!"
MATTHEW 8:23–25

We had some crazy thunderstorms at our house one night while I was working on this book. Shake-the-house crazy! The lightning flashes were so bright and the thunder so loud and powerful, it was pretty scary! In any storms that scare you, remember that Jesus has total power to protect. He can stop a storm with just His words if He chooses to, so of course He can keep you safe.

"He said to them, 'Why are you afraid? You have so little faith!' Then He stood up. He spoke sharp words to the wind and the waves. Then the wind stopped blowing. Then men were surprised and wondered about it. They said, 'What kind of a man is He? Even the winds and the waves obey Him' " (Matthew 8:26–27).

Dear Jesus, You are so powerful to be able to just speak and stop the winds and the waves immediately. I don't ever want to stop being amazed by You! Help me to have great faith and never be afraid! Amen.

Day 188

The Most Epic Fruit Salad Ever

But the fruit that comes from having the Holy Spirit in our lives is: love, joy, peace, not giving up, being kind, being good, having faith, being gentle, and being the boss over our own desires. The Law is not against these things.
GALATIANS 5:22–23

What are your favorite fruits? Apples? Grapes? Bananas? Strawberries? You'd probably have a hard time picking just one because they're all yummy! Each has a unique flavor, and when mixed together, they create one awesome fruit salad.

Because you're a Jesus girl, do you realize you have access to a different kind of fruit? Galatians tells you what "fruits"—godly characteristics—the Holy Spirit (God's Spirit) gives you. When you say yes to Jesus, these fruits begin to grow in you, and you can access them when you need them. Together, they make you a mature Christian who lives and loves well.

What fruit do you need the most? What fruit of the Spirit is the easiest for you? Remember that you can confidently ask God for help plucking these fruits whenever and wherever.

God, thank You for creating in me the most epic fruit salad ever!

Day 189

Solomon's Prayer: Part 1

The Lord came to Solomon in a special dream in Gibeon during the night. God said, "Ask what you wish Me to give you."
1 KINGS 3:5

Solomon loved God, and God gave him an extraordinary opportunity. God came to Solomon in a special dream and told Solomon he could ask Him for anything he wished! Wow!

Here's what Solomon said:

> "You have shown great loving-kindness to Your servant David my father because he was faithful and right and good and pure in heart before You. And You have kept for him this great and lasting love. You have given him a son to sit on his throne this day. Now, O Lord my God, You have made Your servant king in place of my father David. But I am only a little child. I do not know how to start or finish. Your servant is among Your people which You have chosen. They are many people. There are too many people to number. So give Your servant an understanding heart to judge Your people and know the difference between good and bad. For who is able to judge Your many people?" (1 Kings 3:6–9)

Solomon could have asked God for any selfish thing, but he asked to have understanding and to be able to judge right from wrong wisely.

Dear God, help me to be like Solomon and ask You for understanding and wisdom. I want to keep on asking for more and more every day. Amen.

Solomon's Prayer: Part 2

It pleased the Lord that Solomon had asked this.
1 Kings 3:10

God was very happy with Solomon for his request for understanding and said:

> God said to him, "You have asked this, and have not asked for a long life for yourself. You have not asked for riches, or for the life of those who hate you. But you have asked for understanding to know what is right. Because you have asked this, I have done what you said. See, I have given you a wise and understanding heart. No one has been like you before, and there will be no one like you in the future. I give you what you have not asked, also. I give you both riches and honor. So there will be no king like you all your days. And if you walk in My ways and keep My Laws and Word as your father David did, I will allow you to live a long time." (1 Kings 3:11–14)

We can learn so much from Solomon's prayer. When he prayed to know and do what was right according to God's ways, God not only happily gave him great wisdom but also blessed him with great riches and honor!

Dear God, thank You for the example of Solomon and the way You blessed him so much beyond what he expected when he chose to pray for understanding and right judgment instead of selfish things. Amen.

Day 191

Follow His Steps

*The steps of a good man are led by the Lord.
And He is happy in his way. When he falls, he will not
be thrown down, because the Lord holds his hand.*
PSALM 37:23-24

Have you ever fallen down in front of a lot of people? Maybe you tripped on the soccer field or fell down the stairs at school or bumped into someone in the halls and fell flat on your backside. It's so embarrassing when things like that happen and even harder to live through the giggles and comments from those who saw it happen.

God knows we're human, and that means we will fall down in other ways too. He knows we'll make bad choices and do things we know are wrong. He knows we will make sketchy decisions that will get us into trouble. But rather than laugh or shame us, God is there to pick us up and set us on the right path.

Courageously ask God to go before you so you can follow His steps. He will never lead you the wrong way.

....

God, I want to follow You all the days of my life.

The Only Perfect Thing

As for God, His way is perfect. The Word of the Lord has stood the test. He is a covering for all who go to Him for a safe place.
PSALM 18:30

Nothing in this world is perfect. No parent (nope, not even your mom). No friend, classmate, or teammate. No teacher or youth leader. Nothing built or created. No plans or ideas. So if you are looking for perfection from one of these, you're going to end up disappointed.

But there is a place you can find perfection.

Scripture tells us God's will and ways are perfect. It says His Word—the Bible—is perfect. And it teaches that His ability to care for us is perfect. But it takes courage to believe, especially because we are surrounded by people and things that let us down every day.

Do you struggle to trust God? Are you afraid He will let you down or not show up at all? Ask God to give you the faith to know He is always faithful and trustworthy.

God, I know You're the only perfect one anywhere. Give me the courage to trust You!

Day 193

Proactive Prayer

Look to the Lord and ask for His strength. Look to Him all the time.
1 CHRONICLES 16:11

When we were brainstorming ideas for this book, we went to a little café and tried mochi ice cream for the first time. Mochi ice cream is ice cream that's wrapped in Japanese sticky rice dough. Jodi got salted caramel, Lilly got cookies and cream, and I got coconut pineapple.

Lilly took one bite and made a hilarious disgusted face. She didn't like it—not one bit! Her reaction and the funny look on her face made Jodi and me laugh until our sides hurt!

According to wordcentral.com, to react to something means "to act or behave in response."

On the other hand, to be proactive means "to act in anticipation of future problems, needs, or changes."

Lilly's big reaction to the mochi ice cream made us think about how some people pray only as a reaction to life's negative events. Like only praying to God when you're already sick rather than also praying ahead of time to stay healthy. Or only praying to God in emergency situations or natural disasters rather than praying to God all the time in relationship with Him.

Of course we should pray in reaction to life's events. We need God's help! But we should also be strongly *proactive* in our prayers, building a close relationship with God while talking with Him all the time about everything—past, present, and future, not just when we find ourselves in desperate need of help.

Dear God, help me to be a proactively praying girl. Amen.

Brave Enough to Believe

"Do not let your heart be troubled. You have put your trust in God, put your trust in Me also."
JOHN 14:1

In this passage of scripture, Jesus is comforting His followers. He's reminding them that He has their back so they can relax. And even though this reminder is from a long, long time ago, we can also be encouraged by His words today.

It's like Jesus is refocusing you. He is snapping His fingers in front of your sweet face to get your attention. He is reminding you that He knows your worries and is trustworthy to fix them.

Can you remember a time when you prayed about something, felt comforted and encouraged that you'd get through it, and then found yourself freaking out about it again? Rather than trusting God to mend your friendship or fix the situation at home, you started to worry again. You got scared.

Jesus is asking you to put your trust in Him and keep it there.

God, I'm sorry that I stopped trusting You. Please make me brave enough to believe in Your ability to fix the things that worry me.

Day 195

Missionaries Everywhere

"But you will receive power when the Holy Spirit comes into your life. You will tell about Me in the city of Jerusalem and over all the countries of Judea and Samaria and to the ends of the earth."
ACTS 1:8

Missionaries aren't just people who travel the world and live in foreign countries to tell people about Jesus. We are all missionaries everywhere we go and with our friends who are not believers. The Great Commission is for all of us to do as Jesus said: "Go and make followers of all the nations. Baptize them in the name of the Father and of the Son and of the Holy Spirit. Teach them to do all the things I have told you" (Matthew 28:19–20).

Every believer should always be looking for and asking God for opportunities to share our faith and be ready to explain it. But some people (maybe you someday!) do feel called specifically to leave their original countries and go make a new country their permanent home in order to share the gospel of Jesus with the people there. Being a foreign missionary takes a lot of courage, and these individuals need a lot of support.

If you don't already know, find out which missionaries your church supports and commit to praying especially for them. You also might want to write them letters to encourage them and get to know them!

. . . .

Dear God, thank You for people who are willing to travel far away and make their homes in all-new places to share the gospel and help build Your kingdom. Remind me to pray for them regularly! Amen.

Sticky Joy

"You are sad now. I will see you again and then your hearts will be full of joy. No one can take your joy from you."
JOHN 16:22

You are the boss of you. And when it comes to certain things, you're the one who gets to make choices for yourself. You choose whether you get mad or offended when someone says rude things. You get to choose if you are friendly and kind or not. You are the one who decides what your attitude will be for today. And it's you who chooses if joy sticks to you or not.

But let's be honest. Sometimes joy is hard to hold on to. It can start sliding away when you hear a mean rumor about yourself or when you do something embarrassing in front of a crowd. It can unstick when your parents ground you or you forgot the test was today. But sweet one, even with all of these joy killers, you can be brave and choose to let it stick to you instead.

Regardless of your situation, ask God for the courage to make joy stick.

God, help me to have sticky joy no matter what!

Day 197

Healthy Prayers

Give all your worries to Him because He cares for you.
1 PETER 5:7

Jodi and Lilly go to a dentist who only cares for kids, where there are a lot of things to be thankful for: super nice staff, movies to watch on the ceiling while their teeth are examined and cared for, and prizes to choose at the end of the visit. Sometimes I wish there were dentists for grown-ups who did these fun things too!

    No matter what type of doctor visit you may have, you can take time to pray while you are there, giving thanks for the opportunity to receive good medical care. So many people in the world can't afford good care or don't have any dentists or doctors nearby, so simply being able to go to a doctor to help keep you healthy means you are very blessed!

....

Dear God, even if I don't like doctor or dentist visits very much, help me to be thankful for the care I have access to. And You know my body and my health best of all, so please guide medical professionals as they help take care of me. Amen.

More Healthy Prayers

*Don't look out only for your own interests,
but take an interest in others, too.*
Philippians 2:4 NLT

As you're waiting in a doctor's office, it's not okay to ask others what they are there for. That would be too nosy, for sure! But during your wait time, you can look around discreetly and in your mind pray for the people around you. Whether they are there just to get a checkup or to be treated for an illness, they have worries and problems like every person does. Pray that the medical staff will be able to help them and make them feel better quickly. Most importantly, pray that they know the very best Healer of all—Jesus—as their Savior. Who knows how God might answer those prayers!

Jodi, Lilly, and I also like to say a quick prayer anytime we hear a siren from an emergency vehicle like an ambulance or fire truck. In our minds or out loud, we pray, "God, we don't know what that situation is, but You do. Please help the people who are hurt or in danger, and please guide the people who are on their way to help."

Dear God, You know our bodies and our needs better than anyone, and we thank You for how You have gifted medical professionals and rescue workers to be helpers. Please work through them to heal people from sickness and protect people from danger. Amen.

Day 199

Prayer Expectations

"Ask, and what you are asking for will be given to you. Look, and what you are looking for you will find. Knock, and the door you are knocking on will be opened to you."
MATTHEW 7:7

In this verse, Jesus is teaching us how to pray. He is making sure we understand that prayer isn't empty. Sometimes it can seem like our prayers hit the ceiling and bounce back down. We get frustrated because it feels like God isn't answering us quickly enough or isn't responding with what we desperately want. And there are times we want to give up praying altogether because it just doesn't seem to be working.

But Jesus wants you to know that if you have the courage to really seek God, you'll find Him. If you boldly ask for things that don't go against His will for you, He'll give them. And if He says no to any of them, it's only because there's a better yes down the road.

God hears every prayer you pray, so don't give up until He answers.

God, give me strength to seek Your help even when the answer doesn't come right away.

Day 200

Attitude Is Everything

*A glad heart is good medicine,
but a broken spirit dries up the bones.*
PROVERBS 17:22

From the day you were born to the day you see Jesus face-to-face, you're going to face some hard times, mean people, and frustrating moments. It's just part of life, and no one gets through life without feeling broken at times. That's normal. It's to be expected. But you don't have to let yucky things ruin this glorious life!

No matter what life throws your way, you can stand up to it and be okay. You are brave, sweet girl! And attitude is everything.

The happiest people are the ones who look for the silver lining—the good things—when their situation looks ugly. It doesn't mean they don't hurt. They may be afraid. Chances are they'd rather hide under their blankets until things get easier. But rather than live broken, they choose to have a glad heart.

You're not a victim. Courageous girl, you are a victor!

....

*God, I want to see the silver lining in everything.
Help me to have the right attitude no matter what!*

Day 201

Like Talking to a Friend

*Inside the Tent of Meeting, the Lord would speak
to Moses face to face, as one speaks to a friend.*
Exodus 33:11 NLT

There is so much to learn from Moses' life as recorded in the Bible. He had great favor with God, meaning God paid special attention to Moses and delighted in him. Scripture tells us God would speak to Moses face-to-face like one speaks to a friend! Yet later in Exodus 33, we learn that Moses could not look directly at God's face because His glory is just too great! Reading this passage reminds us how awesome our God is and how He wants to be in close relationship with His people.

We can humbly ask to have great favor with God while we respect and follow His Word. Pray like Moses: "If it is true that you look favorably on me, let me know your ways so I may understand you more fully and continue to enjoy your favor" (Exodus 33:13 NLT).

Dear God, I want to make You happy and have Your favor on me. I humbly ask You to delight in me as I obey You. Please help me to grow in Your ways and understand You more every day. Amen.

Day 202

What Label Do You Wear?

God is the One Who makes our faith and your faith strong in Christ. He has set us apart for Himself. He has put His mark on us to show we belong to Him. His Spirit is in our hearts to prove this.
2 CORINTHIANS 1:21–22

Do you ever feel like you're wearing an unflattering label, one that says ugly, stupid, or unlovable? And because you're sure everyone can see that invisible label stuck right to your forehead, it makes you feel insecure. You find yourself nervous that someone might notice the label and make fun of you. You're worried about being rejected and disliked. And rather than enjoy your time at school or with friends, you want to hide instead.

Well, the truth is that you do wear a label—a mark that God has placed on you to show you belong to Him. It's a label that tells how much you are loved, how treasured you are, and how much God delights in who you are! So be confident, because you wear it well.

.....

God, remind me that I'm marked by You and that I'm deeply loved regardless of what others think.

Day 203

Ungrip Those Fists!

"Give, and it will be given to you. You will have more than enough."
LUKE 6:38

I love the example I've heard many times that you can't accept new gifts from God if you keep a tight fist around what you already have. An open hand that shares is one that can receive new gifts. As you receive every kind of gift in life, whether money or a birthday gift or the gift of a special talent, ask God to help you be generous with it and use it in a way that brings praise and glory to Him!

Read and remember these scriptures inspiring us to give and give and give some more!

- "I showed you in all things that you should work as I did and help the weak. I taught you to remember the words of Jesus. He said, 'It is more blessed to give than to receive' " (Acts 20:35 ICB).

- "Don't forget to do good and to share with those in need. These are the sacrifices that please God" (Hebrews 13:16 NLT).

- "Give freely and become more wealthy; be stingy and lose everything. The generous will prosper; those who refresh others will themselves be refreshed" (Proverbs 11:24–25 NLT).

Dear God, please ungrip my fists from the gifts You give me. Help me to love giving and sharing and watching how You give in return. Amen.

Never Alone

"No man will be able to stand against you all the days of your life. I will be with you just as I have been with Moses. I will be faithful to you and will not leave you alone."
JOSHUA 1:5

There's a big difference between being alone and being lonely. When you're alone, you still feel loved and valued. Maybe you need that alone time because it's how you recharge after being with friends all day. Maybe it's when you get your homework or chores done. But lonely is different.

You feel lonely when you believe lies that say you're not lovable. It's when you think no one wants to hang out with you because you're not good enough. It's when you feel left out by your friends, and it makes you question your awesomeness. Those lies of loneliness have the power to knock your self-confidence.

But you can have confidence in this truth: God will never, ever leave you. Even if all your friends ditch you, God never will. There will always be someone with you.

....

God, I need courage to keep my chin up when I feel alone and to remember You're always with me!

Day 205

Keep on Going

We can rejoice, too, when we run into problems and trials, for we know that they help us develop endurance. And endurance develops strength of character, and character strengthens our confident hope of salvation. And this hope will not lead to disappointment. For we know how dearly God loves us, because he has given us the Holy Spirit to fill our hearts with his love.
ROMANS 5:3–5 NLT

Jodi was sick on vacation recently, and it was such a bummer when there was so much fun stuff to do. She was feeling yucky with a fever, but we prayed and God helped her keep on going through the tour we had planned that day. Then later she got to rest and began to feel better.

Even little tests of our endurance let us experience how God gives us strength we don't have on our own. And that builds our faith that He will always provide and help us through tougher times in the future. The next opportunity to build endurance might be a bigger problem or trial. But if we pray and depend on God through every kind of trouble, He will be building our character and hope in Him—hope that will never disappoint us!

Dear God, help me to rejoice in problems and suffering. It's so hard sometimes, but You want me to learn to depend on You through them—and that kind of dependence is such a blessing! Thank You for loving me so well. Amen.

Look at the God Things

*Be full of joy always because you belong to
the Lord. Again I say, be full of joy!*
PHILIPPIANS 4:4

There are plenty of reasons to not be joyful these days. Fights with friends, frustrations with parents, and fears about your grades. There are stresses with schedules, anger at coaches, and annoyances with your siblings. You may worry about a family problem or a disease someone is battling. There's anxiety about fitting in, standing out, and finding the right friends. You may be nervous about making the wrong decisions or not being strong enough to choose the right ones. Unfortunately, there are lots of ways sadness can creep into your heart.

Paul writes in Philippians that your ability to have joy requires one thing, and it's to know you belong to God. That alone should make joy explode in your heart! Because when you focus your attention on the hard things, you can't see the God things. But when you instead look at all the good things about God and how much He loves you, you can find the courage to look away from the things that steal your joy.

....

God, help me to focus on the You things!

Day 207

With Just a Word

"Only speak the word, and my servant will be healed."
MATTHEW 8:8

When we pray, we need to remember the example of the army captain in the book of Matthew in the Bible. He had such great faith that Jesus only had to say the word and his servant would be healed:

> Jesus came to the city of Capernaum. A captain of the army came to Him. He asked for help, saying, "Lord, my servant is sick in bed. He is not able to move his body. He is in much pain." Jesus said to the captain, "I will come and heal him." The captain said, "Lord, I am not good enough for You to come to my house. Only speak the word, and my servant will be healed. I am a man who works for someone else and I have men working under me. I say to this man, 'Go!' and he goes. I say to another, 'Come!' and he comes. I say to my servant, 'Do this!' and he does it."
>
> When Jesus heard this, He was surprised and wondered about it. He said to those who followed Him, "For sure, I tell you, I have not found so much faith in the Jewish nation." . . . Jesus said to the captain, "Go your way. It is done for you even as you had faith to believe." The servant was healed at that time. (Matthew 8:5–10, 13)

Dear God, please grow my faith in You to be as strong as that of the captain in Matthew 8. I know You can just say the word and make a miracle happen! Amen.

Day 208

New Things

*"See, I will do a new thing. It will begin happening now.
Will you not know about it? I will even make a road
in the wilderness, and rivers in the desert."*
ISAIAH 43:19

This truth should encourage you! Sometimes we are desperate for God to do a new thing in our life because the situation we're currently in is so hard. We want a fresh start so we can put bad choices behind us and move on. We're ready to walk a new path with new friends or a new attitude. There are times we crave something new!

What do you need God to make fresh in your life? Do you need different friendships or a new semester to start? Do you need a new relationship with your parents or a better way to handle conflict? God is a God of new things, and you can boldly ask for His help whenever you need it.

....

God, I need help to see the new roads and rivers You're creating for me. Just like You did for Isaiah, I am asking You to do a new thing in my life today.

Brand-New Brain

Take hold of every thought and make it obey Christ.
2 CORINTHIANS 10:5

Have you ever been studying for a big history test and filling your brain with all the little details you need to remember until you're pretty sure it's about to explode with facts and dates and names? You might feel like you need a big mental break after the test is done, right? A total mind renewal or a brand-new brain!

Because we live in a world full of unbelievers, sometimes we spend too much time studying what they do and say and think, and soon that seems to be all that's filling our brains and we even start to copy them. In those moments, we need a brain renewal, and God is the one to give it! His Word says, "Do not act like the sinful people of the world. Let God change your life. First of all, let Him give you a new mind. Then you will know what God wants you to do. And the things you do will be good and pleasing and perfect" (Romans 12:2).

Dear God, when my brain is filling up with the things of this world too much, please refresh me with a new mind that is focused on You and what You want for my life! Amen.

Day 210

The Sound of Joy

*How happy are the people who know the sound of
joy! They walk in the light of Your face, O Lord.*
PSALM 89:15

Are you a complainer? If asked, would your family and friends say you're critical of others? Would they say you nitpick, finding the negatives in situations? Do you whine when you don't get your way or protest when Mom asks you to do chores? Is it easy for you to find fault in the ways others do things? Do you nag your friends or siblings? These are hard questions to face because sometimes we don't even know we're being that way.

But if you want to be happy and enjoy all that life has to offer, then learn to hear the sound of joy. Just what is that? It's the opposite of complaining.

Have the courage to look past the negatives and find the good things instead. With your relationships, your schoolwork, and your extracurricular activities. . .choose to focus on the positives so you can be joyful. And you'll be more fun to be around too!

*God, I want to be a positive person and
spread joy to those around me!*

Day 211

Praying the Names of God

His name will be called Wonderful, Teacher, Powerful God, Father Who Lives Forever, Prince of Peace.
Isaiah 9:6

The scripture above gives some of the names of Jesus, and if you google the words "names of God," you'll find lists of scriptures pointing you to where you can find many more names used for God. Focusing on these names can be so powerful as we become aware of different aspects of our amazing God and the ways He cares for us.

Here are just a few:

- Elohim means Creator God.
- Adonai means Master over All.
- El Elyon means Most High God.
- Jehovah Jireh means The Lord Will Provide.

With your family or by yourself, you could do a cool prayer project of researching and writing down the many names of God used in the Bible. Then study and use those names as you pray! For example. . .

....

Dear Elohim, my Creator God, You are Adonai, Master over All, including being Master over my life and every challenge I face. You care about all my needs because You are Jehovah Jireh and You will always provide! Thank You, El Elyon, the Most High God! Amen

Day 212

Always the Same

Jesus Christ is the same yesterday and today and forever.
HEBREWS 13:8

One of the things we can be certain of is that change will happen. Everything in life changes. Think about it. Next year you'll be in a different grade or maybe a different school altogether. You may be taller and have longer hair, and you'll probably have to buy the next size up in clothes and shoes. Your group of friends may have some new members, and your team will look different too. Change happens.

But God never changes. He is always faithful, always trustworthy, always listening, always forgiving, and His love for you never changes. God is the one you can cling to when change gets scary, because you know He will keep you steady. He will always be 100 percent devoted to you, ready to help when you ask.

The Lord will always be there to help you walk through the changes you'll face in life. Ask, and He will give you the strength to do it well.

....

God, change is hard for me because it's scary. Would You make me brave and help me to accept new things?

Day 213

Help for the Helpless

Religion that is pure and good before God the Father is to help children who have no parents and to care for women whose husbands have died who have troubles.
JAMES 1:27

As a kid you might struggle to know exactly what you can do to help the most helpless in our world, but keep asking God and He will show you. Maybe there's a canned food drive at school or in your community you can give to. Your church probably has several ministries it contributes to and ways kids can help. Sort through your clothes and toys that you don't use anymore that are still in good shape and donate them to shelters. If you know a family who has adopted or does foster care, ask them how you can help. Pray with your parents about whether adoption or foster care is an option for your family. Find a center that helps moms and babies and see if you can help clean or sort items. And keep praying and praying that God will raise up leaders and organizers who truly love and obey Him and want to protect and provide for the most helpless in our world.

Dear God, show me my part in helping the most helpless among us who are all created in Your image and dearly loved by You! Amen.

The Waiting Game

*"The Lord is my share," says my soul, "so I have hope
in Him." The Lord is good to those who wait for Him,
to the one who looks for Him. It is good that one should
be quiet and wait for the saving power of the Lord.*
LAMENTATIONS 3:24–26

No one likes to wait. We want what we want right now, don't we? We want the fight to be over without talking it through. We want grades to change now without having to study more. We're impatient that summer break is months away and cranky that we're grounded for another week. We pray, asking God to fix the situation or heal our broken heart. And so often, the answers come slow, and we think we'll burst because being patient is excruciating.

But this passage of scripture says God is good to those who wait for Him. He loves it when we trust, giving Him space to work things out for us. And God will reward us for waiting on Him.

. . . .

*God, I need strength to overcome my impatience.
Help me to trust that You hear me
and are working on it.*

Day 215

Prayer for Good Friends

Two are better than one, because they have good pay for their work. For if one of them falls, the other can help him up. But it is hard for the one who falls when there is no one to lift him up.
ECCLESIASTES 4:9–10

Whether you like to have a lot of friends or you're happy to have just one or two, you need good friends who encourage you, especially who encourage you to love and obey God. The right kinds of friends are such a blessing. They are iron sharpening iron as Proverbs 27:17 says, which means good friends keep helping each other be and do their best.

If you don't already have friends who love and follow Jesus like you do, ask God to bring them to you. He will, though it might take some time. I've learned that sometimes He wants us to grow closer to Him first through prayer and His Word before He blesses us with a new friend. And if you're already blessed with good Christian friends, thank God and ask Him to keep growing your good friendships!

....

Dear God, thank You for wanting to bless us with wonderful friends! Amen.

Day 216

More Prayer for Friends

Don't fool yourselves. Bad friends will destroy you.
1 Corinthians 15:33 cev

While the Bible encourages you to have good friends, it also warns against having bad friends, like 1 Corinthians 15:33 says. These scriptures caution against bad friends too:

- "Wise friends make you wise, but you hurt yourself by going around with fools" (Proverbs 13:20 cev).
- "Don't befriend angry people or associate with hot-tempered people, or you will learn to be like them and endanger your soul" (Proverbs 22:24–25 nlt).

If you find yourself in some bad friendships, with kids who are encouraging you to get into trouble and move far away from obeying God, you will need courage to get out of those friendships. But you absolutely need to. Ask your parents or a trusted grown-up for help and advice, and believe that God will help you be brave if you ask and depend on Him. And then be ready, knowing that those friends might not like your choices. If they treat you badly, hold on to this truth: "God blesses you when people mock you and persecute you and lie about you and say all sorts of evil things against you because you are my followers. Be happy about it! Be very glad! For a great reward awaits you in heaven" (Matthew 5:11–12 nlt).

Dear God, please help me to be wise about friendships. Amen.

Day 217

The Payoff for Patience

*But they who wait upon the Lord will get new strength.
They will rise up with wings like eagles. They will run and
not get tired. They will walk and not become weak.*
ISAIAH 40:31

In this verse, God is making a very powerful promise. He is telling you the payoff for being patient and choosing to trust that He is making a way for you. God is giving you His word that your patience will bring an awesome benefit: endurance.

What are some of the ways impatience gets the best of you? Do you throw a temper tantrum? Have a pity party? Do you become cranky, making sure everyone pays for your frustration?

How would things be different if you instead decided to bravely wait for God to do what only God can do? And if that big dose of strength you needed to deal with a tough situation was the payoff for choosing to trust God, would you?

God's got this. Your job is to trust Him as you wait.

. . . .

*God, remind me of how faithful You are.
Give me patience as I wait on You.*

A Life Full of Seasons

*There is a special time for everything. There is a time
for everything that happens under heaven.*
ECCLESIASTES 3:1

Life flows in seasons. There are times when it seems everything is clicking, and things feel exciting and easy. Friendships are strong, your family is connecting, and you're content. There isn't much drama or sadness, just happy moments that make your heart feel full. But there are also times when you're overwhelmed by life. Situations are hard and relationships are frustrating, and you just want to curl up in your favorite blanket and cry.

Be ready, courageous girl. Be brave. Because life will often be a roller-coaster ride full of ups and downs. It will be full of good and bad, beautiful and painful. But the one constant will be God. He will be with you through it all. He will cheer you on and wipe away every tear you cry because God is for you and always with you.

It will take courage, but the Lord will give it to you when you need it.

*God, may I lean on You in all the
seasons I'll walk through.*

Day 219

Pray and Provide for the Needy

He who shows kindness to a poor man gives to the Lord and He will pay him in return for his good act.
PROVERBS 19:17

You've probably encountered homeless and needy people, maybe when you've visited a big city or even in smaller towns at intersections where needy people often stand with cardboard signs to beg for food and money. My heart aches for each of these people, and only God knows exactly how they got to this point and exactly what they need.

You can pray for God to give them the shelter and provisions they need, and you can ask God what He wants *you* to do. Talk to your parents about what they would allow you to do to help and how you can help as a family. Maybe you'll want to put together blessing bags full of snacks and water bottles and a Bible plus things like soap and deodorant and socks to pass out when you see a needy person on the streets. Maybe you can volunteer at a shelter. Find out what your church does to help the needy in your community and join in!

Always you can keep asking God to give you compassion and wisdom to come up with good ways to help the needy people around you—and then be ready to obey!

. . . .

Dear God, thank You for my blessings. Help me to share them with those who have so little. Amen.

Day 220

Better Than Anything Else

O taste and see that the Lord is good.
How happy is the man who trusts in Him!
PSALM 34:8

What are your favorite foods? Ice cream or pizza? Steak or chicken alfredo? Banana bread or Caesar salad? Sushi or chili? Think about how much you look forward to eating those foods and how they put a huge smile on your face. Now, remember what it tastes like when you take that first bite. You probably close your eyes and breathe out with pleasure, maybe even sighing loud enough so those around can hear. And remember how happy you are once you're full.

That's the kind of reaction we should have about God. We should crave time with Him and think about our heavenly Father with excitement. We should look forward to connecting and feel happy when we do. Because He is so good—better than anything the world can offer—our hearts should be full when we spend time with Him.

Put God at the top of your menu every day. He is better than anything else!

....

God, I'm determined to crave a relationship
with You above all other things.

Through Everything God Has Made

For ever since the world was created, people have seen the earth and sky. Through everything God made, they can clearly see his invisible qualities—his eternal power and divine nature. So they have no excuse for not knowing God.
ROMANS 1:20 NLT

We like to watch some popular science and nature shows and documentaries. The way God created our world is so cool! But it's sad how unpopular it is to give God credit as Creator. When we watch these shows, we try to remember to pray for the people who make the shows and participate in them. We pray that they will recognize that nothing in our world just happened—it's all part of a wonderful design by our amazing Designer, the one true God! And we pray that they would believe in the one true God and accept Jesus Christ as their Savior.

Anyone you know who helps teach you at school or helps take care of you, like doctors and nurses, might have tremendous knowledge of God's wonderful creation and the scientific world without actually acknowledging God as Creator and Savior. So as you interact with these people, pray that their eyes would be opened to our amazing God!

....

Dear God, You have made Yourself known through every awesome thing and person You have created. Please help more and more people to see that truth and believe in You! Amen.

Day 222

You Are Seen

So Hagar gave this name to the Lord Who spoke to her, "You are a God Who sees." For she said, "Have I even stayed alive here after seeing Him?"
GENESIS 16:13

God sees you. He sees every tear you cry, and He knows all the ways your sweet heart gets broken. God sees those things that bring you joy. He is cheering you on as you take courageous steps forward into tough situations. He knows what scares you. He sees those circumstances that make you feel small. God is fully aware of the people who encourage you and the ones who hurt your feelings. He knows what you need even before you do and has already determined a way to help.

Sometimes we feel unseen even by our closest friends and family. We feel like no one really knows how we're feeling or what we're thinking. We decide we're all alone. But that's not the truth, and we can ask God for the confidence to believe that He sees inside our heart and knows everything that's going on.

God, thank You for knowing me like You do. Remind me that I'm not alone and that You always see me.

Fake Show-Offs

"Two men went to the Temple to pray. One was a Pharisee, and the other was a despised tax collector. The Pharisee stood by himself and prayed this prayer: 'I thank you, God, that I am not like other people—cheaters, sinners, adulterers. I'm certainly not like that tax collector! I fast twice a week, and I give you a tenth of my income.' But the tax collector stood at a distance and dared not even lift his eyes to heaven as he prayed. Instead, he beat his chest in sorrow, saying, 'O God, be merciful to me, for I am a sinner.' I tell you, this sinner, not the Pharisee, returned home justified before God. For those who exalt themselves will be humbled, and those who humble themselves will be exalted."
LUKE 18:10–14 NLT

The Pharisees in the Bible were the rich and snobby religious leaders who were prideful and loved to act like they were better than others. But they were fakes. The above passage from Luke 18 shows that being show-offs didn't reward them at all. It was the humble tax collector who quickly became right with God because he admitted he was a sinner.

Dear God, I don't ever want to be fake and arrogant toward people like the Pharisees were. Help me to be confident and sincere in who You made me to be, and help me to confidently share Your truth with others.

Day 224

Courageous Asks

*God is able to do much more than we ask or
think through His power working in us.*
EPHESIANS 3:20

God's power and ability are endless. Think about it. He can do anything He wants. God can make anything happen at any time. And He can dream bigger than we can ever imagine. We may ask for the cupcake, but He can give us the entire bakery!

What do you need God to do? Where do you need Him to show up in your life? What are you asking Him for? This is your challenge to ask for more. Ask bigger. Ask for things only God can make happen. Be courageous in your prayers, and boldly ask Him for your heart's desire.

At the same time, be brave enough to accept God's answer. Sometimes He answers over and above what we asked, and other times He requires us to wait as He lines things up. And there are also times His answer is no because there is something better right around the corner. Regardless, be fearless in your asks.

*God, help me to be fearless and bold
in the prayers I pray to You!*

Day 225

Pray to Be Humble

Pride ends in humiliation, while humility brings honor.
Proverbs 29:23 nlt

God's Word talks a lot about not being proud but instead being humble, but what does that mean exactly? It means not thinking of yourself as better than other people. It means being teachable, knowing you can always keep learning from others and never trying to be a know-it-all. It doesn't mean you can't have any confidence or be happy with your accomplishments, but as a humble Christian, you'll place your confidence in God's work within you, recognizing that He alone gives you the ability to accomplish any good thing!

Read and remember these scriptures, and pray for God to keep your heart humble before Him.

- "The heart of a man is proud before he is destroyed, but having no pride goes before honor" (Proverbs 18:12).

- "So humble yourselves under the mighty power of God, and at the right time he will lift you up in honor" (1 Peter 5:6 nlt).

Dear God, I want to be humble and teachable and give You credit for everything in a world where that's not usually the cool thing to be and do. Please help me. I want to make You happy and trust that You bless and reward and lift me up when I depend completely on You! Amen.

What Are You Focusing On?

We do not look at the things that can be seen. We look at the things that cannot be seen. The things that can be seen will come to an end. But the things that cannot be seen will last forever.
2 Corinthians 4:18

This verse offers a powerful tip. It's saying a key to living a happy life is to not focus on the problems we face. Rather than freak out that our family is in crisis or that we're moving across the country, we instead focus on God. We say, "This is scary, but I trust that whatever You're doing is for the best!"

Refocusing isn't easy, especially when everything seems to be going wrong. It's hard to trust when your grades are failing, your friendships are frustrating, and your motivation is falling apart. It's hard to stay out of the drama! But if you can find the courage to step back, take a deep breath, and talk to God about it, you'll be able to focus on the right things.

....

God, keep my eyes on You when life gets hard. Help me to trust that You have everything under control!

Day 227

Be Able to Laugh

*Live and work without pride. Be gentle and kind.
Do not be hard on others. Let love keep you from doing that.*
EPHESIANS 4:2

One way you know you might have too much pride and need more humility is if you can never laugh at yourself. Ephesians 4:2 says not to be hard on others—and so you shouldn't be hard on yourself either! Every single one of us is going to make silly mistakes. Or do clumsy things. Or say something dumb we thought might be funny but then totally wasn't. I've done so many of these things I could never keep track of them all. If I have too much pride, I might never be able to get past them or show my face around the people who witnessed them. But if I choose to act humbly and laugh it off and apologize if needed, I can move on, knowing that I am fully loved and forgiven by God and that my identity and confidence are in Him.

So pray for God to give you a good sense of humor in those moments when you need to humbly laugh at yourself and move on. His Word says, "A cheerful heart is good medicine, but a broken spirit saps a person's strength" (Proverbs 17:22 NLT). Life's mistakes and embarrassing moments are bound to happen, but you never have to let them break your spirit!

....

*Dear God, help me to be humble enough to laugh at myself
and move on from mistakes and embarrassing moments,
trusting that I am fully loved and cared for by You! Amen.*

When Are You Quiet?

*"All of you be quiet before the Lord.
For He is coming from His holy place."*
ZECHARIAH 2:13

The world is loud, and many of us like it that way. We love our music and the laughter from our friends. We love to watch our favorite shows and sit around the dinner table talking with our family. Youth group and team sports are times when we interact with others, and before we go to sleep, we're on our phones squeezing out every last bit of conversation.

But do you ever make time to sit quietly with God? Without music or conversation, do you find moments when it's just you and God? He has so much to say to you, but it requires you to listen for His voice. If your attention is always somewhere else, how will you hear Him?

Starting today, why not schedule time to sit in silence with God and listen for His voice? He has things to say. Will you listen?

....

God, may I be firm in my commitment to spend time with You quietly. Please meet me there and speak to my heart.

Pray to Learn from Mistakes

Pride leads to disgrace, but with humility comes wisdom.
PROVERBS 11:2 NLT

Another way to be a humble person without pride is to be grateful for mistakes because of what they can teach you. Together with a group of young dancers, Jodi and Lilly recently helped lead worship through dance at our church on a Sunday morning, and a lot of people were in attendance. When Lilly made a small mistake in the dance, at first she felt so embarrassed. But she didn't let it stop her from dancing and worshipping. She kept going, with a beaming smile on her face and arms and legs and body moving in wonderful praise to our amazing God!

What if after she messed up she instantly ran off the stage in embarrassment? That would have been super distracting to the whole worship time. So choosing to move on from the little mistake and focus on going forward doing her best—instead of running away—was definitely the right decision. And even though she cried a few tears afterward to her dance leader and to me, she learned what a good thing it is not to let embarrassing mistakes crush your spirit or stop you from worshipping or doing what God has planned for you. Instead, you can be humble, learn from your mistakes, and keep living, dancing, loving, and bringing God glory!

. . . .

Dear God, I constantly need to pray for Your help to be humble, to admit mistakes, and to be willing to learn from mistakes. Teach me the lessons that You want me to learn when I mess up. Thank You so much for always loving me, no matter what. Amen.

The Power to Meet Needs

He lets me rest in fields of green grass. He leads me beside the quiet waters. He makes me strong again. He leads me in the way of living right with Himself which brings honor to His name.
PSALM 23:2-3

The twenty-third Psalm is one of the most popular passages of scripture in the Bible because it shows us God's power to meet our needs. Every one of us has moments when we desperately need what these verses offer. Reread the verses out loud. Which parts speak to you the most? Why?

It's important to remember that no matter your age, race, location, or anything else, God is always available. He doesn't listen to one person before another person because He doesn't have to. When you cry out to Him, you have 100 percent of His attention. And somehow at the very same time, anyone who prays to God also has His full attention.

That means when you need rest, direction, courage, or strength, God hears you the moment you ask Him for it.

....

God, thank You for always being there to meet every one of my needs.

Day 231

Our Daily Fight

Our fight is not with people. It is against the leaders and the powers and the spirits of darkness in this world. It is against the demon world that works in the heavens. Because of this, put on all the things God gives you to fight with. Then you will be able to stand in that sinful day. When it is all over, you will still be standing. So stand up and do not be moved. Wear a belt of truth around your body. Wear a piece of iron over your chest which is being right with God. Wear shoes on your feet which are the Good News of peace. Most important of all, you need a covering of faith in front of you. This is to put out the fire-arrows of the devil. The covering for your head is that you have been saved from the punishment of sin. Take the sword of the Spirit which is the Word of God.
EPHESIANS 6:12–17

Every day each of us should wake up remembering we're in the middle of a fight. That doesn't need to scare us because God never, ever leaves us. He wants us to fight hard and stand firm against evil in the world. We do this by putting on and using all the armor God has given us like the scripture above tells us.

....

Dear God, help me to be on guard each day in the fight against evil in this world. I want to keep standing strong for You! Help others to see my faith in You and want to join in fighting sin and evil. Amen.

Day 232

Created and Molded

*But now, O Lord, You are our Father. We are the clay,
and You are our pot maker. All of us are the work of Your hand.*
ISAIAH 64:8

God created you. Period. If you believe the Bible to be completely true, then settle this fact in your mind today. God is the one who thought you up. He decided what you would look like, when and where you'd be born, what family you would grow up in, and all the talents He'd give to you. God took His time to form you just right.

Even now, God continues to mold you into the person He has planned for all along. Every hard thing you face, God uses for your benefit. And even the joy-filled times are used to develop you too. From friend drama to being cast as the lead in the school play, God is directly involved in your life. And now that you understand He has His fingers in every part of your life, you can confidently choose to trust Him no matter what.

. . . .

Heavenly Father, thank You for making me. . .me!

Worship with Song and Prayer

Come, let us sing with joy to the Lord. Let us sing loud with joy to the rock Who saves us. Let us come before Him giving thanks. Let us make a sound of joy to Him with songs. For the Lord is a great God, and a great King above all gods. The deep places of the earth are in His hand. And the tops of the mountains belong to Him. The sea is His, for He made it. And His hands made the dry land. Come, let us bow down in worship. Let us get down on our knees before the Lord Who made us. For He is our God.
PSALM 95:1–7

Do you have favorite worship songs that you especially love? Awesome if you do! I hope you stop to really focus on the lyrics sometimes. You could even write them down in your prayer journal if you're keeping one. Think about the lyrics and make them both a song and a prayer to God. And even during times when you're not able to listen to music, ask God to help the words and tune stick in your mind and let your mind go to them when you're needing encouragement and a boost in your faith.

. . . .

Dear God, I want songs of praise to You to fill my mind all the time! Amen.

Wherever You Go

"See, I am with you. I will care for you everywhere you go. And I will bring you again to this land. For I will not leave you until I have done all the things I promised you."
GENESIS 28:15

There are few people that promise to be with you through thick and thin. Most parents would make that kind of pledge. So would your bestie. There might be a mentor or two or a small-group leader. But no one can totally make that promise because life is so unpredictable.

That's why God's promise to be with you everywhere you go is so awesome! Without fail, you can always count on God to be available when you need Him. He will always care for you and give you the things you need to get through your day. And there is nothing you can do to make Him mad enough to leave you. God is incapable of abandoning you.

Find time today to tell God what this promise means to you.

....

God, what would I do without You?
I'm so glad You will never leave me.

Day 235

Sticky Scripture

I think about your orders and study your ways. I enjoy obeying your demands. And I will not forget your word. Do good to me, your servant, so I can live, so I can obey your word. Open my eyes to see the wonderful things in your teachings.
PSALM 119:15–18 ICB

Worship songs are great to have stuck in your head, and even better are the exact words of scripture. And you can sing them as songs too, of course! Ask God to help scripture be sticky in your mind when you hear it and read it. It's a prayer He loves to answer, and so often He'll bring to mind exactly what you need in encouragement and truth at exactly the right moment. His Word is how He wants to guide you and teach you, and He is so happy when you listen and obey! Romans 15:4 says, "Everything that was written in the Holy Writings long ago was written to teach us. By not giving up, God's Word gives us strength and hope."

Dear God, as I read and listen to and learn Your Word, please make the scriptures extra sticky in my mind. I never want them to get out! Amen.

Who Do You Trust More?

*"Good will come to the man who trusts in the Lord,
and whose hope is in the Lord. He will be like a tree planted
by the water, that sends out its roots by the river. It will not
be afraid when the heat comes but its leaves will be green.
It will not be troubled in a dry year, or stop giving fruit."*
JEREMIAH 17:7–8

Every day, you have a choice to make. You can put your trust in people, or you can instead decide to trust God. And honestly, it's a hard choice to make. But when you put your faith in God, not only will you grow, you'll also have the strength and courage necessary to take the next right step.

This passage in Jeremiah gives the perfect example of what trusting God looks like and how having faith saves you. Just like the tree planted by the water, you will have access to resources to help you get through the dramatic moments of life. And that's something only God can give you.

*God, give me the boldness I need to trust
You over anyone else. You are faithful!*

Day 237

Special Gifts

We all have different gifts that God has given to us by His loving-favor. We are to use them. If someone has the gift of preaching the Good News, he should preach. He should use the faith God has given him. If someone has the gift of helping others, then he should help. If someone has the gift of teaching, he should teach. If someone has the gift of speaking words of comfort and help, he should speak. If someone has the gift of sharing what he has, he should give from a willing heart. If someone has the gift of leading other people, he should lead them. If someone has the gift of showing kindness to others, he should be happy as he does it.
Romans 12:6–8

God has given you special gifts and talents that He wants you to use to help spread His love and bring Him praise! Maybe you have already figured out what some of those gifts are, and you might discover more as you're growing up. Pray for God to give you confidence in the gifts He has given you and ask Him for opportunities to share them well!

. . . .

Dear God, help me to know my special gifts You've created me with. Show me how You want me to use them. May they point many people to knowing and loving You! Amen.

Day 238

Blessing from Waiting

I did not give up waiting for the Lord. And He turned to me and heard my cry. He brought me up out of the hole of danger, out of the mud and clay. He set my feet on a rock, making my feet sure.
PSALM 40:1–2

What kind of trials and hard times have you faced? We've all had something. Maybe it was the loss of a family member or friend, fear that you might be sick, rejection from someone you love, or horrible consequences from a bad choice. Everyone has been in the pit before, just waiting and hoping to be rescued. And chances are those pits have taught you some good things.

It's the time we spend waiting in those hard places that brings about blessings. We become stronger or smarter. We learn to be more compassionate and loving. We find a deeper faith in God. Or we realize we're braver than we thought. Sometimes God allows the pit to be a classroom only because He will use it to help us grow. And when the timing is perfect, He pulls us from it.

God, help me to see the blessings that come from waiting.

Day 239

Prayer for Contentment

I have learned to be happy with whatever I have. I know how to get along with little and how to live when I have much. I have learned the secret of being happy at all times. If I am full of food and have all I need, I am happy. If I am hungry and need more, I am happy. I can do all things because Christ gives me the strength.
PHILIPPIANS 4:11–13

In his letter to the Philippians, the apostle Paul teaches us a wonderful thing to pray for and tells us how to have it: contentment. In a world with such cool stuff plus the internet that tells us all about it instantly, we often struggle to be content with the life we've been given. It's easy to look at other people's stuff and what they do and where they go on vacation and want all of it instead of or in addition to the good things we already have. We have to pray hard against envy and greed and remember like Paul how to be happy and content. We simply have to remember that we can do all things through Christ who gives us strength. Because He helps us, we can be happy and endure when we have too little and we can be happy and give thanks when we have plenty. Jesus gives us strength no matter what, and trusting in Him is where real contentment comes from!

....

Dear God, please help me to be content with whatever You decide to bless me with and to trust in Your strength and the ways You provide, no matter what I have or don't have. Amen.

Day 240

You're Kind of a Big Deal

But you are a chosen group of people. You are the King's religious leaders. You are a holy nation. You belong to God. He has done this for you so you can tell others how God has called you out of darkness into His great light.
1 PETER 2:9

Courageous girl, you are kind of a big deal. Think about it: Your Father is the Creator of the heavens and earth. He is the King of kings and the Lord of lords. He is and always has been. And there is none greater than God. And that makes you royalty.

According to Peter, you are chosen. That means handpicked. You are holy because you belong to God and He is holy. And He has given you a voice to tell others about what He has done in your life. You're His spokesperson.

Be brave enough to walk in the truth. Others might try to cut you down and make you feel worthless, but remember who you are. Because of God, you are kind of a big deal.

God, thank You for being such an amazing heavenly Father! I love You so much.

Best Use of Time

So be careful how you live. Live as men who are wise and not foolish. Make the best use of your time. These are sinful days.
Ephesians 5:15–16

It's super easy to get distracted or to be lazy about doing the good work God has for us to do. What are the things that tempt you away from doing the things you should be doing (like time with God, schoolwork, chores around the house, etc.)? Television? Video games? Social media? Those things aren't necessarily all bad, but we need to pray and have discipline so they don't get in the way of what's most important in our lives. And what's most important in our lives should be what Jesus said the greatest command is: " 'You must love the Lord your God with all your heart and with all your soul and with all your mind.' This is the first and greatest of the Laws. The second is like it, 'You must love your neighbor as you love yourself.' All the Laws and the writings of the early preachers depend on these two most important Laws" (Matthew 22:37–40).

And then we keep asking Him to show us how to live carefully and wisely, making the best use of our time and using our gifts to glorify Him in all the things He has planned for us to do.

. . . .

Dear God, help me to keep Your great commandments first in my life—loving You completely and loving others as myself. Then help me to manage my time wisely to bring the most glory to You! This is a prayer I'll need to keep praying again and again—thank You for hearing and helping me! Amen.

Day 242

Time to Move On

No, Christian brothers, I do not have that life yet. But I do one thing. I forget everything that is behind me and look forward to that which is ahead of me. My eyes are on the crown. I want to win the race and get the crown of God's call from heaven through Christ Jesus.
PHILIPPIANS 3:13–14

It's time to let go of what you have done and instead grab on to what God is doing in your life moving forward. We've all done shameful things and have made wrong choices. We've all been mean to friends and rude to family members. We may have cheated on a test or stolen something from a store without getting caught. But having faith and trusting in God gives us the ability to leave those in the past and focus on our relationship with Jesus.

Ask God for the courage to not dwell on the ways you've failed. Because of Jesus' death on the cross, you've been forgiven for every bad choice. Now it's time to move forward and concentrate on building a strong relationship with Jesus.

God, thank You for fresh beginnings!

Day 243

Pour Out Your Heart

*As we have suffered much for Christ and have shared
in His pain, we also share His great comfort.*
2 CORINTHIANS 1:5

Think about a time when you've felt rejected. Maybe someone you thought was a good friend excluded you and hurt you and ended the friendship. Maybe you tried out for a school play, positive you'd get a great role, but then didn't get any part at all.

In hurtful, confusing times like these, pour out your heart to God in prayer. He wants to pull you close and comfort you and remind you that Jesus knows exactly what it's like to feel rejected. He knows and He cares. When you share with Him in suffering, you are bonding with Him, and He's developing your faith and your character and also storing up rewards for you in heaven.

So keep trusting and loving our Savior and keep praying, no matter what rejection and suffering you go through. He is good through it all, and He is working to make all things right!

....

Dear Jesus, when I feel rejected, remind me how rejected You were–so rejected that people beat You and then killed You on the cross. But that sure wasn't the end. In Your rejection and suffering God was working to save the world. Remind me that You are working in ways I don't know yet when I am rejected and suffering too. Please comfort me and strengthen my faith as You work behind the scenes! Amen.

Day 244

Take Pride in Your Work

*Whatever work you do, do it with all your heart.
Do it for the Lord and not for men.*
COLOSSIANS 3:23

You were created to work—we all were. When God thought you up, He decided what gifts and talents you would get and how they would benefit those around you. It's easy to grumble about work, whether it's schoolwork or a job you're paid to do. Sometimes we'd rather be doing anything but the work right in front of us. But if you look at work as an act of worship instead, it could change your attitude.

Ask God to help you value working. Take pride in making good grades, and care about the papers you have to write. Put all your effort into the class presentation, and be prepared for the game. Memorize your part in the play, and perfect your choir or band solo. Do these things to make God proud and to show Him you are thankful for the skills He has trusted you with.

. . . .

God, I want to honor You in my work. Thanks for blessing me with the ability to do things well.

Day 245

Jonah's Prayer

The Lord sent a big fish to swallow Jonah.
JONAH 1:17

What's the worst, most bizarre way you can think of that your parents might discipline you for disobedience? I'm guessing Jonah in the Bible never imagined he'd wind up in the belly of a giant fish! But he did end up there because he didn't obey God. And inside that fish, he prayed:

> "I called out to the Lord because of my trouble, and He answered me. I cried for help from the place of the dead, and You heard my voice. You threw me into the deep waters, to the very bottom of the sea. . . . But You have brought me up from the grave, O Lord my God. While I was losing all my strength, I remembered the Lord. And my prayer came to You, into Your holy house. Those who worship false gods have given up their faith in You. But I will give gifts in worship to You with a thankful voice. I will give You what I have promised. The Lord is the One Who saves."
>
> Then the Lord spoke to the fish, and it spit Jonah out onto the dry land. (Jonah 2:2–3, 6–10)

Dear God, help me to learn from Jonah that there are always negative consequences for disobeying You. Thank You, though, for still loving and caring for Your people when they make mistakes and for hearing and answering their cries for help when they repent and want to obey You again. Amen.

The Focus of Life

*"I am the Vine and you are the branches.
Get your life from Me. Then I will live in you and you will
give much fruit. You can do nothing without Me."*
JOHN 15:5

There are lots of people who think being good is the goal of life. In their own strength, they work hard to treat people kindly, save seats for friends at lunch, volunteer at Vacation Bible School, and offer to be the teacher's helper in class. While those things are worthwhile, alone they won't make your life perfect. Even more, your strength will eventually run out, and you'll become bitter that you're having to work so hard.

But Jesus says the focus of your life should be having a relationship with Him. It's from that connection that we can bless and serve others. We will be able to access His strength and grace to be kind to those around us. We can access His courage to love those who are hard to love and forgive those who are hard to forgive. Staying close to Jesus is how we live a beautiful and fulfilling life.

God, I'm choosing to stick with You!

Day 247

Prayer When Grieving

O Lord my God, I cried to You for help and You healed me.
PSALM 30:2

If someone you love has ever died very suddenly, you might know, like we do, that it's an awful shock to lose someone with zero warning. Losing a loved one in any kind of way, whether you have a chance to say goodbye or not, is heartbreaking. But we've learned and experienced how God gives extra special grace and care when we stay close to Him and let Him heal our broken hearts—even when we don't fully understand Him. We stayed close to Him through His Word and through prayer, crying out to Him with all our grieving emotions, including sadness, anger, fear, and confusion. And we have been amazed at how He has comforted and provided in many different ways.

If you are grieving the loss of a loved one, keep crying out to God and reading His Word. Tell Him everything you are feeling, even the angry and confused feelings, and ask for His help. Search His Word and let Him show you how He will heal your heart, giving you His love through many different sources and people.

Dear God, please hold me extra close when I am grieving and missing a loved one. I don't understand, but I don't want to turn away from You. Please comfort me and heal my heart and grow my faith in You. Amen.

What Anchors You?

*This hope is a safe anchor for our souls.
It will never move. This hope goes into the Holiest
Place of All behind the curtain of heaven.*
HEBREWS 6:19

Who are the anchors in your life? You know, the people who hold you steady. Is it your friends? Your parents? Maybe an older sibling or a small-group leader. Maybe an aunt or uncle. Or maybe you anchor yourself to the idea of being perfect or being an overachiever. We all rely on different anchors to help us make sense of this crazy world.

But God is the only safe anchor because we can confidently place our hope in Him. We can trust that He will always keep us close and safe. He will be there whenever we need help or wisdom, courage or strength, peace or comfort. While we may be loved by some pretty awesome people here on earth, it's God's love that's able to move mountains on our behalf. And when we make the bold decision to tie our life to Him, He will protect us.

....

*God, my hope is anchored in You. Help me to
stay connected to You above anyone else.*

Day 249

A Test for God?

"Bring to the storehouse a tenth of what you gain. Then there will be food in my house. Test me in this," says the Lord of heaven's armies. "I will open the windows of heaven for you. I will pour out more blessings than you have room for."
MALACHI 3:10 ICB

You don't normally think of getting to give your teacher a test, do you? Well, God is the greatest teacher of all, and there is one way He actually wants us to give Him a test! It's by seeing how much He gives to us in return when we choose to be cheerful givers to Him. Start while you are young and make a habit your whole life of giving at least one-tenth of the money you earn back to God. Remember, any ability you have to work comes from God anyway, and simply giving 10 percent of it is a wonderful way to thank Him. You get to keep 90 percent! This giving is called tithing.

How do you tithe money to God? By giving to churches and ministries that teach His Word and serve and care for people like Jesus did, in His great name. And giving to others as you see they have needs. Time and time again, God will bless you for doing so. It's not always in terms of money that He will give back to you (though sometimes it is) but also in ways like special opportunities and close relationships and good health and unexpected treats and on and on! Test Him and see, praying for Him to show you as you do.

Dear God, show me how much You love to give to me when I love to give to You! Amen.

Day 250

Desperate Prayers

I call to You from the end of the earth when my heart is weak. Lead me to the rock that is higher than I. For You have been a safe place for me, a tower of strength where I am safe from those who fight against me. Let me live in Your tent forever. Let me be safe under the covering of Your wings.
Psalm 61:2–4

Can you hear the writer's desperation in this verse? It's obvious he's in a pretty rough spot and in need of God's help. Can you relate?

Think back to a time when you were at the end of your rope. Maybe you were in an epic fight with your parents and felt unheard. Maybe there was a rumor at school that wouldn't die down and you were embarrassed. Maybe your best efforts in class weren't paying off and your grade suffered. Maybe you're in a desperate place right now.

If there's anything to learn from the psalmist, it's that God is willing and able to help when you need it, but you have to be courageous enough to reach out.

. . . .

God, hear my desperate prayers and help me. I need You.

Choose with Care

Test everything and do not let good things get away from you. Keep away from everything that even looks like sin.
1 Thessalonians 5:21–22

We sure have a lot of options in movies, television, music, and social media these days. And so we have all the more reason to pray for wisdom about what we watch, listen to, read, and participate in on the internet. We should strive to be able to say, like David did in Psalm 101:1–5 (NLT):

> I will sing of your love and justice, Lord. I will praise you with songs. I will be careful to live a blameless life—when will you come to help me? I will lead a life of integrity in my own home. I will refuse to look at anything vile and vulgar. I hate all who deal crookedly; I will have nothing to do with them. I will reject perverse ideas and stay away from every evil. I will not tolerate people who slander their neighbors. I will not endure conceit and pride.

Dear God, please give me wisdom as I make media and social media choices. Sometimes the options seem so out of control for girls my age, and it's sure not a popular choice to be careful! But I love You, and I want to stay away from anything that causes me to sin and disappoint You. Amen.

It's a Sure Thing

*"Do not fear, for I am with you. Do not be afraid, for I am your
God. I will give you strength, and for sure I will help you.
Yes, I will hold you up with My right hand that is right and good."*
ISAIAH 41:10

God promises to step in when we ask. Where do you need His help today? Are you struggling and scared? Are your feelings hurt? Do you need courage or wisdom to do the next right thing? Are you feeling weak? Unlovable or unlikable? Unworthy? Overwhelmed? Stressed-out? Sometimes this life just beats us up. But sweet one, never forget that God sees you right where you are.

Did you notice in today's verse where He says He will "for sure" help when we need it? That means He will without a doubt be there for you. It means nothing will stop God from getting involved. He is ready and willing to act on your behalf. Your challenge is to be fearless in asking for His help.

. . . .

*God, I know You're there for me, but sometimes I struggle to ask
for help. Please give me the courage to reach out.*

Lighthouse Lesson

*This is the day that the Lord has made.
Let us be full of joy and be glad in it.*
PSALM 118:24

Once while in Florida, we were all excited to climb up the steep stairs inside a historic lighthouse and see the beautiful views from the top. But when we got there, we learned Lilly wasn't quite tall enough to be allowed to climb up. We were all bummed we were unable to go together, Lilly especially! Maybe you've had something like this happen to you.

Sometimes life is like that. There are age limits and rules to follow that we might not fully agree with or understand or that we might be disappointed by. But we have a choice how we respond in those frustrating situations. We can choose to pout and be grumpy, or we can choose to have a good attitude. The lighthouse situation was hard for Lilly at first, but soon she was choosing to have a good attitude and also to be grateful for the blessing that day—she was given a free pass to come back and climb the lighthouse in a year or so when tall enough. We haven't had a chance to get back there and use that pass yet, so she still has that blessing to look forward to!

. . . .

Dear God, please help me when I need to accept limits and rules that I don't like or don't understand. May I choose a good attitude even when I'm frustrated. Amen.

Day 254

You Can Go to God for Anything

*Let us go with complete trust to the throne of God.
We will receive His loving-kindness and have His
loving-favor to help us whenever we need it.*
HEBREWS 4:16

You can go to God for anything, at any time, no matter what. Even more, you can pray to Him with complete trust, knowing that He will hear you and respond. Your friends and family may have the same good intentions because they love you so much, but only God can meet your needs 100 percent of the time. Only God is available right when you need Him. And He is the One who holds every answer and solution in His hands.

So. . .what do you need from God today? More patience with your siblings? Compassion for that annoying classmate who won't give you space? Wisdom to know how to talk to your mom about something that's bothering you? Confidence for the big game? Courage to stand up for yourself? Ask God. He's waiting to hear from you.

*God, I need Your help today. I'm thankful that
I can talk to You about anything and that
You already have the answers I need.*

Head in the Clouds

Keep your minds thinking about things in heaven.
COLOSSIANS 3:2

God has wonderful plans for each of our lives on earth! Ephesians 2:10 (ICB) says, "In Christ Jesus, God made us new people so that we would do good works. God had planned in advance those good works for us. He had planned for us to live our lives doing them." But God doesn't want us to get too attached to our lives here on earth because they are not our forever lives with Him in heaven. First John 2:15–17 (NLT) says, "Do not love this world nor the things it offers you, for when you love the world, you do not have the love of the Father in you. For the world offers only a craving for physical pleasure, a craving for everything we see, and pride in our achievements and possessions. These are not from the Father, but are from this world. And this world is fading away, along with everything that people crave. But anyone who does what pleases God will live forever."

We need to keep the perspective of finding joy and purpose in the good plans for which God has created us while remembering that our life on earth is temporary and our forever home is in heaven.

. . . .

Dear God, thank You for the good plans You created me for here on earth. Help me to walk closely with You and do them for Your glory. And thank You for promising that someday I will live forever in a perfect heaven! Amen.

Day 256

What to Do When Others Are Mean

My times are in Your hands. Free me from the hands of those who hate me, and from those who try to hurt me. Make Your face shine upon Your servant. Save me in Your loving-kindness.
PSALM 31:15–16

Life can be hard, and people can be so mean, leaving you feeling hopeless, like things will never be okay. It's difficult to understand how people can be so hurtful, especially when it's on purpose. And it leaves us feeling unloved and scared.

One of the best things to do when you're overwhelmed by the meanness of others is pray. God is able to change the situation as well as the hearts of people trying to hurt you. He can make it stop. And because God sees everything, there is nothing happening to you that He's missed. He knows exactly what's going on, and God is waiting for you to ask for His help. Be bold and tell God what you're feeling and what you need. He's listening.

. . . .

God, I am struggling. I'm sad about how others are treating me. I need Your help right now.

Day 257

Job's Prayer of Praise

There was a man in the land of Uz whose name was Job. That man was without blame. He was right and good, he feared God, and turned away from sin.
Job 1:1

Job's faith in God was tested in such an incredibly difficult way. It's hard to even imagine the pain and sorrow he endured. Yet after losing so much, including his livestock, his servants, and all his children, "Job stood up and tore his clothing and cut the hair from his head. And he fell to the ground and worshiped. He said, 'Without clothing I was born from my mother, and without clothing I will return. The Lord gave and the Lord has taken away. Praise the name of the Lord.' In all this Job did not sin or blame God" (Job 1:20–22).

We can follow Job's example in this prayer, and no matter what God gives to us or takes away from our lives, we can trust and worship God through it all.

Dear God, help me to have faith and endurance like Job so that no matter what hard things I have to go through, I will choose to trust and praise You. Amen.

Day 258

Job's Prayer of Repentance

"He who speaks strong words against God, let him answer."
JOB 40:2

If you read the whole book of Job, you will find that as it goes on, Job was tested even more and he did not continue to praise God through it all. In fact, he had quite angry words for a while. But in the end, after God reminded Job of His greatness and goodness, Job cried out in repentance, telling God how sorry he was:

> "I know that You can do all things. Nothing can put a stop to Your plans. 'Who is this that hides words of wisdom without much learning?' I have said things that I did not understand, things too great for me, which I did not know. 'Hear now, and I will speak. I will ask you, and you answer Me.' I had heard of You only by the hearing of the ear, but now my eye sees You. So I hate the things that I have said. And I put dust and ashes on myself to show how sorry I am." (Job 42:2–6)

We need to learn from Job that when we cry out to God with angry words, we should stop and realize that God's power and love and control over all things are beyond our understanding. And we need to say we are sorry for disrespecting God. After Job repented, God blessed him again even more than he had been blessed in the first place!

....

Dear God, help me to learn from Job that if I speak in anger to You, I need to say I'm sorry and continue to trust in You. Amen.

Prayer: A Weapon against Lies

*Let the lying lips be quiet. For they speak with
pride and hate those who do right and good.*
PSALM 31:18

Few things hurt more than having lies spread about you. Whether it's a friend betraying you or someone you barely know starting the rumor, lies cut deep. And they usually spread like a wildfire, circulating from one person to the next at record speeds. Even more, it's so hurtful that people who know you would choose to believe whatever they're told. But the hardest part may be finding the courage to walk the halls when you know others are gossiping about you.

People usually talk bad about one another because doing so makes them feel better about themselves. They fuel mean-spirited rumors because they're jealous or angry. And unfortunately, at some point in your life—if you haven't already—you will be the victim of a liar.

But there's hope. Prayer is a weapon you can use anytime, and sometimes it takes everything you've got to step out of the hurt to pray to the Healer. But when you do, God will help.

....

God, I'm hurting. Please give me peace and strength.

Day 260

Who's the Boss?

*If your sinful old self is the boss over your mind,
it leads to death. But if the Holy Spirit is the boss
over your mind, it leads to life and peace.*
ROMANS 8:6

Keeping your thoughts in check is a full-time job. It's easy to focus on bad things happening rather than what's going right. The frustrating moments can easily overshadow the good ones. Think about it. If five friends compliment you on your outfit and just one person says it's ugly, which one do you remember?

God wants to be the boss of your mind. He wants you to listen to His voice above all else. Instead of letting your mind focus on all the negatives in the situations you're facing, choose to look for where God is moving. Be courageous and stand up to those bad thoughts. Tell them to pack their bags and leave. Don't let them be the boss of your mind, because they will ruin your day.

What bad thoughts do you need to kick to the curb?

....

*God, please be the boss of my thoughts and show
me the ones I need to let go of right now.*

Our Unchanging God

Jesus Christ is the same yesterday and today and forever.
HEBREWS 13:8

We've had a whole lot of change in our lives in the last few years, and it hasn't always been easy. Can you think of a time when you've experienced major change? What were your thoughts and emotions and prayers like during that time?

Nothing in life will always stay the same, and that's why we can be so thankful that God gave us Jesus, who is always dependable and always the same—yesterday, today, and forever! Psalm 102:25–27 says of God, "You made the earth in the beginning. You made the heavens with Your hands. They will be destroyed but You will always live. They will all become old as clothing becomes old. You will change them like a coat. And they will be changed, but You are always the same. Your years will never end."

Our all-powerful God is never going to let us down. So lean on Him and ask Him to hold you steady when life seems to swirl around you with new and unanticipated circumstances. Talk to Him about every joy and sorrow and stress.

....

Dear God, thank You for never changing or letting me down through all life's ups and downs! Amen.

Day 262

Did You Check with God?

*There are many plans in a man's heart,
but it is the Lord's plan that will stand.*
PROVERBS 19:21

This verse isn't suggesting that you not make plans. Truth is, it's important to take steps forward and have hopes and dreams for the future.

There may be a certain college you want to go to or places you want to travel to when you get older. You may have a career in mind, like becoming a lawyer, nurse, singer, or dancer. God gave you a brilliant mind to think for yourself and make plans, and He also gave you a big dose of hope for things to come. Part of growing up is learning how to make wise choices.

But what this verse is suggesting is that you hold these plans loosely because God may have something else in mind. Something better. Something bigger. Something different. Your challenge is to be confident enough to make plans, faithful enough to ask God if He agrees, and courageous enough to set them aside if God shows you another path.

....

*God, I am excited for my future! And I want
to make decisions about it with You!*

Day 263

Good Gifts

"You fathers—if your children ask for a fish, do you give them a snake instead? Or if they ask for an egg, do you give them a scorpion? Of course not! So if you sinful people know how to give good gifts to your children, how much more will your heavenly Father give the Holy Spirit to those who ask him."
LUKE 11:11–13 NLT

Have you ever played with Bunch O Balloons, the kind of water balloons attached together so you can fill up a whole bunch at once? Jodi and Lilly have fallen in love with those this summer as we've been writing this book. They love to take them on the trampoline and slip and splash while they jump. Their dad went to the store the other night and surprised them by bringing home some more because they love them so much. And then, as a bonus surprise, the package had a contest code and we won some *more* Bunch O Balloons that will come in the mail sometime soon.

This made me think of the scripture in Luke 11. Great dads do love to surprise their children with good gifts. Moms do too! And our heavenly Daddy loves it so much more than earthly parents do. So it's totally okay to ask your heavenly Father for good gifts!

Dear God, thank You so much for wanting to bless me with good gifts. I am so grateful! Amen.

Day 264

It Doesn't Matter What They Think

*The fear of man brings a trap, but he who
trusts in the Lord will be honored.*
PROVERBS 29:25

It's easy to worry about what others think. We become people pleasers because we want to be liked. Our heart can ache for the seal of approval from certain people. We become overwhelmed by focusing our time and energy on making sure we're loved by everyone around us. It's exhausting. Even more, the writer of Proverbs 29:25 tells us that worrying too much about the opinions of others is a trap.

Based on your own life, can you see that? Can you recall times you cared more about what *they* thought rather than courageously following what God was asking of you? The writer goes on to say that if you will boldly trust God and follow His way instead, He will honor you. In other words, if you make the hard choice to care about God's will over the approval of anyone else, you'll be rewarded. It takes guts and grit, but you can do it.

....

*God, give me courage to not care so
much about what others think.*

Day 265

Anna, a Woman of Prayer

Anna was a woman who spoke God's Word. She was the daughter of Phanuel of the family group of Asher. Anna was many years old. She had lived with her husband seven years after she was married. Her husband had died and she had lived without a husband eighty-four years. Yet she did not go away from the house of God. She served God day and night, praying and going without food so she could pray better. At that time she came and gave thanks to God. She told the people in Jerusalem about Jesus. They were looking for the One to save them from the punishment of their sins and to set them free.
Luke 2:36–38

We hope you like to learn about historical women. Even though they lived so long ago, the women of the Bible who loved God should still inspire us today! One of these is Anna, a woman you can look up to and model your life after. She had lost her husband yet wanted to serve God wholeheartedly and pray all the time. She was delighted when Jesus was born and praised God because she knew Jesus would be our Savior.

....

Dear God, help me to be like Anna, serving You no matter what and wanting to pray more and more to grow ever closer to You. Amen.

God Protects His Girls

*"The robber comes only to steal and to kill and to destroy.
I came so they might have life, a great full life."*
JOHN 10:10

There is an enemy who hates you. *Hate* is a pretty strong word, but it's true. The devil has plans for your life, and they are to steal your happiness, kill your joy, and destroy your hope. Don't let that scare you, courageous girl. Remember, you're the daughter of the Most High King, who has amazing plans for your future! But you need knowledge so you understand what the devil wants for you.

When you say yes to becoming a Jesus girl, you're protected by Him. It doesn't mean life will be perfect and without yucky times and messy situations, but it does mean that when you courageously hold on to Jesus, you are a victor—not a victim. No matter what you face—mean girls, bad grades, divorced parents, or a scary sickness—with Jesus you win because He will make the bad things work in your favor.

....

*God, help me to be brave when I am overwhelmed
by the devil's plans. I trust You!*

Day 267

Prayer for Your Country

Pray for kings and all others who are in power over us so we might live quiet God-like lives in peace. It is good when you pray like this. It pleases God Who is the One Who saves.
1 TIMOTHY 2:2–3

You might hear your parents or other grown-ups talking a lot about politics or hear about politics at school. It can be confusing and frustrating, for sure, to understand what's going on and to discern which politicians might be good leaders for our nation. Since you're a kid and can't vote, you might think there's nothing you can do, but there is always something. You can pray, of course! Pray for the leaders of our nation, the president and vice president and their families and all elected officials in federal, state, and local government and their families too. Praying for so many people might seem overwhelming, but you could think of the American flag as a reminder. Every time you see it, pray something like this:

....

Dear God, please bless our nation according to Your will. Help our leaders want to acknowledge and honor You. Please give them Your wisdom to govern well. May each of them know You as the one true God and Savior. Please protect our nation and protect our freedom to worship You, and help us to use that freedom to spread Your truth and love. Amen.

Day 268

Prayer for the World

"Be still, and know that I am God! I will be honored by every nation. I will be honored throughout the world."
PSALM 46:10 NLT

You can pray specifically for each state in your country too. Put a map on a wall somewhere in your house; use it as a visual to remind you to pray, and pick a state to pray for each day. You could also make a chart listing people you know in each state and remember them in extra-special prayer the same day you pray for their state.

And don't just stop there. God loves everyone everywhere in the whole world, not just our nation. Get a globe and start praying for every person in every country and for nations to honor the one true God and to do His will according to His Word.

. . . .

Dear God, You love all people of all nations, and You want them to honor You and trust Jesus as Savior so You can give them eternal life. You are such a good and loving heavenly Father. Help me to remember to pray for all people everywhere! Amen.

Day 269

Scared of the Dark?

This is what we heard Him tell us. We are passing it on to you. God is light. There is no darkness in Him.
1 JOHN 1:5

Are you scared of the dark? Does it make you feel anxious or all alone? When your parents say good night and turn off the light as they leave your room at bedtime, does the darkness feel overwhelming? It's okay if it does. The dark can cause fear, worry, and anxiety.

You may be afraid of the literal dark, but you can also be scared of those dark times in life when you're overwhelmed. Fights, fears, and frustrations have a way of blocking the light right out of life.

But God is light. He's the opposite of the dark. There's not one bit of blackness in Him. Nothing negative, hurtful, scary, or mean-spirited. So when you get scared, the best thing you can do is pray, because when you do, your prayers are bringing light into those dark places. Ask Him to shine His light into your heart and your situation.

God, Your light makes me fearless.
Please help me to look to You when I am scared.

The Old Switcheroo

"You planned to do a bad thing to me. But God planned it for good, to make it happen that many people should be kept alive, as they are today."
GENESIS 50:20

This verse should make you smile ear to ear. It's the hope you can hold on to when bad things happen to you. When mean girls try to make your life miserable, when hurtful rumors are being spread about you, or when someone is picking on you, remember that their mean-spirited plans will fail in the end.

God promises to take all the cruel intentions of others and do a switcheroo. Sure, it might upset you right now, but good will eventually come from it. Maybe the mean girls will make you more confident, the rumors might help you become more courageous, and the one picking on you may become your best friend. Yes, God is capable of changing any situation to work in your favor. Your job is to trust Him to be faithful when you ask for His help.

....

God, when people do things to hurt me on purpose, remind me that You'll use it for good things.

Day 271

Bread of Life

Jesus said, "I tell you the truth, Moses didn't give you bread from heaven. My Father did. And now he offers you the true bread from heaven. The true bread of God is the one who comes down from heaven and gives life to the world." "Sir," they said, "give us that bread every day." Jesus replied, "I am the bread of life. Whoever comes to me will never be hungry again. Whoever believes in me will never be thirsty."
JOHN 6:32–35 NLT

Think about what things in your home you can't imagine living without. Indoor plumbing? Electricity? Air conditioning? Wi-Fi? We are very blessed with modern conveniences today! But our most basic daily needs for life are food and water, right? We couldn't survive long without them. So does Jesus say in this scripture He expects us to believe in Him and never eat food or drink water again? No, but Jesus does want us to trust in Him as the one who provides for all our needs. *He* is our most basic need for life because He is the giver of life—eternal life!

Dear Jesus, thank You for being the giver of life! I trust in You, and You are everything I need. Amen.

God Comforts

Yes, even if I walk through the valley of the shadow of death, I will not be afraid of anything, because You are with me. You have a walking stick with which to guide and one with which to help. These comfort me.
PSALM 23:4

Comfort is one of the sweetest gifts that God makes available to us, because, let's be honest, life is hard. Sometimes it feels like we're constantly dealing with difficult or frustrating things, and that stirs up fear and anxiety.

We worry we'll never fit in at the new school, scared they won't like us. We're afraid to embarrass ourselves during the class presentation, terrified we'd never live it down. We fear rejection from our friends or betrayal from someone we love and trust, and our heart is stirred up and troubled.

God isn't okay with that, so He promises to bring comfort right when we need it the most. Courageous girl, ask for it. Whenever your heart feels anxious, no matter where you are, boldly ask God to comfort you. . .and He will.

God, I'm going to stand up for myself and ask for Your help when I need it.

Pray the Psalms

The Lord is right and good in all His ways, and kind in all His works. The Lord is near to all who call on Him, to all who call on Him in truth. He will fill the desire of those who fear Him. He will also hear their cry and will save them. The Lord takes care of all who love Him. But He will destroy all the sinful. My mouth will speak the praise of the Lord. And all flesh will honor His holy name forever and ever.
PSALM 145:17–21

Anytime you open the book of Psalms, you can read and pray and be encouraged by all the poetic passages that are prayers and praises to God. They are full of honest emotion as the writers pour out their hearts to God, and they can inspire you to do the same. There is nothing you need to hide from God. If you have sin in your life, confess it to Him and make it right. If you are hurting, tell God and let Him comfort you. If you are in need or a loved one is, ask God for His help. If you are scared, let God remind you of His power and protection. If you are full of gratitude and praise, tell Him again and again!

Dear God, help me to remember to turn to the Psalms often and be inspired by honest prayer and praise. Amen.

Day 274

Give Yourself a Break

*But as for me, I will watch for the Lord. I will wait for
the God Who saves me. My God will hear me.*
MICAH 7:7

Give yourself a break. You don't have to be perfect. Chances are the only one expecting perfection from you. . .is you. There's no reason to beat yourself up for being human. God made you, and He thinks you're pretty amazing even when you mess up.

Now, that's not an excuse for bad behavior. Instead, it's a reminder that you aren't expected to have it all together. There is grace for you! Ask God for the courage to accept that you're flawed and lovable at the same time.

Throughout your life, you're going to make countless mistakes. We all will. But God promises to be with you the whole time. Your Father in heaven won't leave you or forsake you because you do something wrong. And when you do mess up, ask God for help and forgiveness, and watch for Him to make things right.

....

*God, thank You for letting me be imperfect.
Give me the confidence to accept it myself.*

Day 275

Bow Down

Then Ezra praised the Lord, the great God, and all the people chanted, "Amen! Amen!" as they lifted their hands. Then they bowed down and worshiped the Lord with their faces to the ground.
NEHEMIAH 8:6 NLT

Maybe you've learned to always bow your head, close your eyes, and fold your hands to pray, and that posture is good to help you focus on God. But really there is no specific position you have to pray in because you never have to stop praying to God. You can be sitting or standing or raising your hands, and you can be anywhere at all when you pray. But sometimes it's good to position your body in a way that reminds you of God's total greatness and your total respect for, devotion to, and need for Him.

If you don't already, you can start bowing your head and kneeling before God beside your bed at night. At our girls' group at church, we have been so encouraged on Wednesdays when we spend a little time on our knees to pray and worship God together, ages kindergarten through fifth grade plus teen and adult female leaders. What a blessing to participate in prayer this way, with a full room of girls and women who want to know and love God better!

....

Dear God, help me to remember that I can pray to You anywhere I am, but I also want to remember to bow and kneel before You at times because I respect and love You so much. I am so grateful to be a child of the King of all kings! I worship You, my Creator, my Savior, and my awesome God! Amen.

Hindsight Is Twenty-Twenty

We want you to know, Christian brothers, of the trouble we had in the countries of Asia. The load was so heavy we did not have the strength to keep going. At times we did not think we could live. We thought we would die. This happened so we would not put our trust in ourselves, but in God Who raises the dead.
2 CORINTHIANS 1:8–9

In today's verse, Paul is on the other side of his struggles in Asia, which gave him the ability to look back and see the bigger picture. Have you ever heard the phrase "Hindsight is twenty-twenty"? Simply put, it means that when you look back at a situation, you're able to understand it better now than when you were right in the middle of it.

Can you think of a tough situation that made sense once it was over? Something with a friend? A parent? A teacher? Maybe God allowed that hard moment because He used it to open your eyes or your heart to Him.

....

God, give me the courage to learn from my circumstances and see You in them.

Day 277

Guard Your Heart

*Guard your heart above all else,
for it determines the course of your life.*
PROVERBS 4:23 NLT

If you've ever gotten a really nasty illness, you probably wanted to figure out what caused it so that hopefully you never have to endure it again, right? Just like we need to be aware of what's going on with our bodies and any aches or illnesses we might have, we need to be aware of our thoughts and emotions and what's causing them, whether good or bad.

If you feel great love for your siblings most of the time, awesome! But if you feel great anger toward them most of the time, not so awesome, right? If you feel sad some of the time, that's understandable. But what if you feel sad *all* the time? Not good! You need to figure out where confusing and overwhelming emotions are coming from and how to communicate about them plus hopefully work out what's causing them. Ask your parents and trusted grown-ups for help and be totally honest about your feelings. And never forget that God knows your heart best of all, and He can help you with everything you feel. Pray to Him and ask Him to give you great wisdom when it comes to your thoughts and emotions and actions and how they all interact.

. . . .

Dear God, sometimes I have a lot of confusing emotions that I'm not sure what to do with. You know my heart and every thought and feeling even better than I do. Can You please help me to sort them out and communicate them well? I also need people like my parents and others who are good at this to help me too. Thank You for caring about every detail of me, God! Amen.

The Safest Place to Be

So give yourselves to God. Stand against the devil and he will run away from you. Come close to God and He will come close to you. Wash your hands, you sinners. Clean up your hearts, you who want to follow the sinful ways of the world and God at the same time.
JAMES 4:7–8

The safest place for you to be is with God. You find that closeness when you pray to Him, read the Bible, listen to praise music, and spend quiet time listening for His voice. He is your safe place when things feel scary and overwhelming. And when it seems everything is falling apart, tucking away with God is the best place to ride out the storms.

He will give you courage so you don't give in to the devil's tricky plans. He will give you strength to face every challenge that comes your way. He will give you bravery to stand up for yourself. And God will give you determination to do the right things.

....

God, with Your help I can stand strong against the devil's plans. You're my safe place.

Day 279

Standstill

On the day the LORD gave the Israelites victory over the Amorites, Joshua prayed to the LORD in front of all the people of Israel. He said, "Let the sun stand still over Gibeon, and the moon over the valley of Aijalon." So the sun stood still and the moon stayed in place until the nation of Israel had defeated its enemies. Is this event not recorded in The Book of Jashar? The sun stayed in the middle of the sky, and it did not set as on a normal day. There has never been a day like this one before or since, when the LORD answered such a prayer. Surely the LORD fought for Israel that day!
JOSHUA 10:12–14 NLT

Amazing! Joshua prayed for the sun and moon to stand still to give extra daylight in order for God's people to win the war against their enemies the Amorites. And God answered in a way He had never done before and has never done again. When you have a huge prayer request, you can think about this story of Joshua and let it build your faith. God is able to command anything in His creation to obey His Word. So surely He is able to help you with every one of your needs, as well as those of your family and friends!

....

Dear God, please remind me constantly of Your all-powerful ways over all creation! No problem is too big for You! Thank You for telling me that I can bring every concern I have to You. Amen.

Day 280

The Weapons of Strength and Peace

*The Lord will give strength to His people.
The Lord will give His people peace.*
PSALM 29:11

God promises that He will give you strength and peace, two very powerful weapons to have in your arsenal. Strength is what gives you courage to do the next right thing, and it's peace that tells your heart that things will be okay. It whispers that God is with you.

Can you think of a situation you're in right now where you need both of these? Maybe it's frustration with a teammate or coach, or maybe a friendship feels unsteady. Maybe there's tension at home, and it has you worried and confused about what to do. Maybe you need to speak up for yourself but are scared it might backfire instead of help. Tell God how you're feeling, and ask Him to bring strength and peace.

You may really want to hide away and try to ignore the things that stress you out, but God wants you to grab hold of these weapons so you can thrive!

．．．

God, I'm so glad I can have strength and peace! Would You give me the right dose of each at the right time?

Demanding Daisy

*O LORD, our Lord, your majestic name fills the earth!
Your glory is higher than the heavens. . . . When I look at the
night sky and see the work of your fingers—the moon and the
stars you set in place—what are mere mortals that you should
think about them, human beings that you should care for them?*
PSALM 8:1, 3–4 NLT

We laugh at our little dog Daisy because pretty much anytime we're in the kitchen, she comes in barking in such a demanding way she seems to be saying, "Give me a treat *now*!" She especially loves little slices of apple, but she'll eat almost anything if we let her.

Do you ever get what you want by demanding things from others? I hope you don't. That's rude and disrespectful. We should never demand things of God either. We should come to Him humbly and with total respect. Don't be like our demanding Daisy to anyone, and especially not to God!

Dear God, may I never be demanding and rude when I ask others for things. Please forgive me and help me to make it right when I mess up and do that. And may I never be demanding toward You. I trust that You always want to give me what's best for me, and I humbly ask You to do so. Amen.

Day 282

You Are a Light

Jesus spoke to all the people, saying, "I am the Light of the world. Anyone who follows Me will not walk in darkness. He will have the Light of Life."
JOHN 8:12

You are a light. God has given you the ability to shine Him into the world. That means your words and your actions can be so amazing that those around you want to know your secret. They'll want to be your friend because you make them feel good. They'll be drawn to your kindness and courage, they'll see your wisdom and strength, and they'll want that for themselves.

Think of three people who need God in their life. Is one of them your friend who is struggling with self-worth? Is one of them a new kid desperate for someone to hang out with? Is one of them a sibling making bad choices or a parent trying to fix everything on their own? Ask God what you can do to shine Him into their lives. Think of ways you can be a light for them.

....

God, give me the eyes to see people who need to know about You, and give me the courage to shine!

Remember

*My voice goes up to God, and I will cry out.
My voice goes up to God and He will hear me.*
PSALM 77:1

Sometimes God answers our prayers by telling us to *remember* because He wants us to focus on what He has done and how He has provided in the past. In Psalm 77, the psalmist starts out troubled and crying and asking questions and wondering if God has forgotten him. But then his tone changes and he prays, "I will remember the things the Lord has done. Yes, I will remember the powerful works of long ago. I will think of all Your work, and keep in mind all the great things You have done. O God, Your way is holy. What god is great like our God? You are the God Who does great works" (Psalm 77:11–14).

So if you're waiting for an answer to prayer, maybe God would like you to remember as you wait. And rather than worry about your current or future needs, you can fill your mind with praise as you recall how God has worked in the past! Then you'll be building your faith strong for how He's helping you now and how He will continue to help you in the future.

. . . .

Dear God, I never have reason to doubt You because all I have to do is remember all You have done in the past. May Your will be done now and in the future too. I will wait on You and trust in You. Amen.

Day 284

You're in Good Hands

"I am the First and the Last. I am the beginning and the end."
REVELATION 22:13

Read today's verse out loud. What a powerful reminder that God always has been and will always be. He is at the start and the finish line and everything in between. There is no place He can't go or space He can't fill. He is fully present, fully available, fully involved. There is nothing and no one bigger or better than God.

So what does this mean for you? It means you're in good hands. It means there is nothing you're dealing with that God cannot fix or help with. He has the unique ability to understand your struggle from every angle and has already made a way for you. It means you can take a deep breath knowing He has everything you need right in this moment. God has you, courageous girl.

How does this truth make you feel? How does it change how you see hard times? What does God want you to know?

....

God, it makes me feel good to know You have everything under control. Give me courage to trust You when hard times hit.

Questions on Repeat

God has said, "I will never leave you or let you be alone."
HEBREWS 13:5

Once when Lilly was three years old, we were at a hotel in Virginia Beach, and she was afraid to go down the short tunnel slide into the pool. She finally did it (with arm floaties securely in place!), but only with her daddy waiting at the bottom to catch her. And before every trip down she had a list of questions she called down the tube to her daddy:

- *"Are you there?"*
- *"Are you ready?"*
- *"Are you sure?"*
- *"Will you catch me?"*
- *"Do you promise?"*

Every. . .single. . .time, she asked these five questions in exactly the same way before she would go down the slide, and every single time her daddy assured her the answer to all of them was yes. She must have done this at least twenty times, and it's a sweet memory we will never forget.

We like to think of this story in relation to the way we call on our heavenly Daddy in prayer. He absolutely answers yes to all these questions too, and He won't get tired of answering—even zillions of times! He's always there, always ready to help, always sticking to His promises, always so glad to hear from us in prayer.

Dear God, thank You for loving me so well. Amen.

Day 286

Do You Doubt God's Greatness?

The Lord is great and our praise to Him should be great. He is too great for anyone to understand. Families of this time will praise Your works to the families-to-come. They will tell about Your powerful acts. I will think about the shining-greatness of Your power and about Your great works. Men will speak of Your powerful acts that fill us with fear. And I will tell of Your greatness.
PSALM 145:3–6

Did you notice the word *great* is mentioned six times in today's verses? It's obvious the writer wants to make that truth clear—the truth that God is great. Why do you think he's so desperate for us to know it? Maybe it's because there are times when we doubt it.

It's hard to stay positive about God when life goes wrong. When everything seems to be falling apart, we often question God's goodness. We wonder why He doesn't save us from the mess or make relationships easier.

But we don't often get those answers. Instead, we need to find the courage to believe God is great no matter what.

God, I know You are great!

Suddenly Swimming

Be strong with the Lord's strength.
EPHESIANS 6:10

During that same trip to Virginia Beach, Jodi had just turned six years old and was trying to overcome some of her own fears, and particularly to swim without arm floaties. I kept encouraging her to take them off, but she didn't want to. Then after a pool break, she went back to the water, got halfway down the slide, and then discovered she had forgotten to put her floaties back on! There was no turning back! She hit the water, which was over her head, and was forced to just start swimming—and she totally did! She was a mix of scared, relieved, and super excited after she climbed the steps out of the pool and came to tell us what had happened.

Sometimes in life we are just unexpectedly thrown into things we think we don't know how to do. Sometimes God lets that happen on purpose so we can get over our fears and to show us He wants us to depend on Him for His help. He is always there, and we can always call on Him in prayer. We might be surprised at what we are capable of with His power working in us!

Dear God, sometimes I find myself unexpectedly thrown into situations where I don't have a clue what to do! Help me to realize how much I can depend on You and Your power in those times. Teach me and strengthen me, please, God! Amen.

Hold Tight to the Truth

As you have put your trust in Christ Jesus the Lord to save you from the punishment of sin, now let Him lead you in every step. Have your roots planted deep in Christ. Grow in Him. Get your strength from Him. Let Him make you strong in the faith as you have been taught. Your life should be full of thanks to Him.
COLOSSIANS 2:6–7

God has plans for your life, ones He thought up before the creation of the world, and He will equip you to walk them out. That means God will give you everything you need to do what He's planned, and He's promised to be with you every step of the way. When He thought you up, God filled you with skills and talents that would grow and mature into awesomeness. There's no doubt you are a rock star!

Don't let anything take that from you. Remember, God created you to be unique on purpose, and the strength you need to thrive comes from God alone. Have the courage to hold that truth tightly.

....

God, help me to grow in You. Help my faith to be strong. Help me to trust You always.

Day 289

God's Greatness

God's riches are so great! The things He knows and His wisdom are so deep! No one can understand His thoughts. No one can understand His ways. The Holy Writings say, "Who knows the mind of the Lord? Who is able to tell Him what to do?" "Who has given first to God, that God should pay him back?" Everything comes from Him. His power keeps all things together. All things are made for Him. May He be honored forever. Let it be so.
ROMANS 11:33–36

Keep Romans 11:33–36 in mind every time you pray. God's riches and power and thoughts and ways are so far above and beyond anything you can possibly imagine. So pray big, telling God you know that nothing is impossible for Him to do, yet humbly asking according to His will. And keep wanting God to grow your faith in Him no matter what His answers to prayer are.

Dear God, remind me to focus on how awesome You are. My mind can't fully understand You, but I want to grow closer to You and honor You. Please strengthen my faith in You and my relationship with You every day of my life. Amen.

Day 290

Are You Angry at God?

*"Agree with God, and be at peace with Him.
Then good will come to you."*
JOB 22:21

When bad things happen, so often we get mad at God. We blame Him for all the things that have gone wrong. We decide He doesn't really love us or He doesn't see us, or we think He is a mean god. While those kinds of thoughts may be normal when our heart is breaking, they are not reality.

God can take your anger. If you're struggling with frustration toward Him right now, tell Him. He's big enough to handle it and willing to hear the things you're feeling. And once you get it all out, once you put it all on the table, God will be ready to put His peace in your heart.

Don't let another day go by without talking to Him. It may take every bit of courage in you, but you are free to confidently share your honest feelings because nothing you say will ever change how much He loves you.

....

*God, I want to live at peace with You!
Would You help me to work through my anger?*

Day 291

Safe in God's Care

God is our safe place and our strength. He is always our help when we are in trouble. So we will not be afraid, even if the earth is shaken and the mountains fall into the center of the sea, and even if its waters go wild with storm and the mountains shake with its action.
Psalm 46:1–3

How do you feel about thunderstorms? What's the scariest experience you've had in one? I'm not a big fan because of all the damage I know they can do. I'm thankful for a basement to go to when storms are raging outside. Psalm 46:1–3 is a wonderful passage to memorize and recite on repeat during a scary storm or any kind of disaster or emergency. We are always safe when we are in God's care. He is our Strength and our Help in times of trouble.

. . . .

Dear God, I have nothing to fear because You keep me safe. Please help me to remember that You are my safe place, even during the loudest thunderstorms or worse. Thank You for Your strength and help. Amen.

Be Bold in Your Faith

Then Nebuchadnezzar became very angry and called for Shadrach, Meshach, and Abed-nego. And they were brought to the king. Nebuchadnezzar said to them, "Is it true, Shadrach, Meshach and Abed-nego, that you do not serve my gods or worship the object of gold that I have set up? Now if you are ready to get down on your knees and worship the object I have made when you hear the sound of the horns and harps and all kinds of music, very well. But if you will not worship, you will be thrown at once into the fire. And what god is able to save you from my hands?"
Daniel 3:13–15

It's hard to stand strong when others think your faith is silly. We don't want to be made fun of, so we keep our belief in God tucked away so no one can see it.

But God is calling you to be a modern-day Shadrach, Meshach, and Abed-nego and to be bold about your relationship with Him. It's never something to be ashamed about. No. It's something to be confident and proud of.

....

God, I am not going to hide how much I love You anymore!

Marvelous Masterpiece

For we are God's masterpiece. He has created us anew in Christ Jesus, so we can do the good things he planned for us long ago.
EPHESIANS 2:10 NLT

I love to talk with Jodi and Lilly as they dream about the many things they might do as grown-ups. And this scripture is one we've memorized and think about as we pray for their futures. God has created each of us as a marvelous masterpiece with good plans for us in mind, so we pray this way—and you can too. . .

....

Dear God, thank You for creating me totally unique. Even my fingerprints are unlike those of any other person in the world. That's so cool! I believe You have good plans for me and good works You want me to do, and I believe my life will be best when I'm following those plans and doing those works! Will You please show and guide me every day? Even now while I'm so young, please put desires in my heart and mind that match the things You want me to do. Please help my schoolwork and the activities I choose to prepare me for those things too. Please open doors of opportunity You want me to walk through and close doors You don't want for me. I want to live a life of serving You and following Your will for me. I believe that is the most rewarding kind of life! Amen.

Day 294

Faith under Pressure

"If we are thrown into the fire, our God Whom we serve is able to save us from it. And He will save us from your hand, O king. But even if He does not, we want you to know, O king, that we will not serve your gods or worship the object of gold that you have set up."
Daniel 3:17-18

Yesterday we read how the king threatened to throw Shadrach, Meshach, and Abed-nego in the fire for not worshipping him. We learned about the bold faith these three carried in their hearts. Today we watch them walk it out.

It's one thing to believe and another thing to believe under pressure. Just like these men did, we have to trust God's plan on such a deep level. They were going to love God whether He saved them from the fire or not. Their faith was solid.

What about you? Do you have a "no matter what" faith? It takes guts to trust God regardless of when or how He answers your prayers. Ask Him for faith under pressure so it can't be shaken.

....

God, I choose to trust You no matter what.

Life's Little Joys

Be happy in your hope. Do not give up when trouble comes. Do not let anything stop you from praying.
ROMANS 12:12

One of our favorite things about summer is a local hot air balloon festival. There is just something so delightful about seeing a sky full of brightly colored balloons. We'd love to visit New Mexico someday and see the Albuquerque International Balloon Festival, the largest hot air balloon event in the world!

What are some of your favorite simple joys? Jodi and Lilly shared they love spending time with family and our dogs and even just looking at the stars in the night sky.

I hope you have many simple things that bring you joy. A lot of sad and stressful things happen in this life, but God doesn't want us to be defeated by them (Romans 12:21). I believe He gives us little things to delight in to help us through those hard times. And ultimately our joy doesn't depend on the situation we're going through; it depends on whether we know Jesus as Savior. With Him as our source of joy, we never run out of it!

Dear God, all my hope is in You, and all my joy comes from You! Thank You for the all the little joys of life until one day we have constant, perfect joy forever in heaven with You! Amen.

Day 296

Faith in the Middle

Then they took him out of the city and threw stones at him. The men who were throwing the stones laid their coats down in front of a young man named Saul. While they threw stones at Stephen, he prayed, "Lord Jesus, receive my spirit." After that he fell on his knees and cried out with a loud voice, "Lord, do not hold this sin against them." When he had said this, he died.
ACTS 7:58–60

Stephen was stoned to death for his faith. He had been encouraging others to follow the Lord, and it made some religious leaders angry, so they dragged him out of the city and threw rocks at him until he died.

You'll probably never see something so brutal happen just for believing, but you may be made fun of for being a Jesus girl. That's okay. People can be mean. But find the courage to be fearless when the mocking comes, having strong faith in the middle of the mean words. Don't allow anyone to make you turn your back on God, because He promises to never turn His back on you.

....

God, I am Your girl. I will be fearless in my faith!

Day 297

More Joy and Hope

Your faith will bring thanks and shining-greatness and honor to Jesus Christ when He comes again. You have never seen Him but you love Him. You cannot see Him now but you are putting your trust in Him. And you have joy so great that words cannot tell about it. You will get what your faith is looking for, which is to be saved from the punishment of sin.
1 PETER 1:7–9

The Bible talks a lot about real joy that comes from knowing God and trusting Jesus as Savior. If you're ever feeling blue and need some extra reminders about joy, read and hold on to these scriptures:

- "Be full of joy always because you belong to the Lord. Again I say, be full of joy!" (Philippians 4:4).
- "You will show me the way of life. Being with You is to be full of joy. In Your right hand there is happiness forever" (Psalm 16:11).
- "If you obey My teaching, you will live in My love. In this way, I have obeyed My Father's teaching and live in His love. I have told you these things so My joy may be in you and your joy may be full" (John 15:10–11).

Dear God, when I'm feeling down, please remind me of the many reasons I have to be full of joy–most of all because of You! Amen.

Day 298

Worry Is a Waste of Time

Jesus said to His followers, "Because of this, I say to you, do not worry about your life, what you are going to eat. Do not worry about your body, what you are going to wear. Life is worth more than food. The body is worth more than clothes."
LUKE 12:22–23

Do you worry? It's easy to get freaked out about little things and big things alike. We're worried because we're afraid something bad will happen. We imagine horrible outcomes and endings, and it keeps us awake at night. It makes it hard to focus at school. Worry can feel overwhelming.

But Jesus tells us worry doesn't belong in our life. He says it's a waste of our time because we end up focusing on the *what if* rather than the *what is*. If we truly trust God, then we shouldn't worry. Instead, we must bravely choose to trust He'll work it all out—even the things that feel scary.

Where do you need to trust God today?

....

God, worry is a waste of time, and I need Your help to get rid of it. Help me to trust You more!

Day 299

Building UP

But you, dear friends, must build each other up in your most holy faith, pray in the power of the Holy Spirit, and await the mercy of our Lord Jesus Christ, who will bring you eternal life. In this way, you will keep yourselves safe in God's love.
JUDE 1:20–21 NLT

If you build a Lego tower with just a single skinny column of bricks, you can build it really tall, right? But it's not very strong and topples easily. But if you build it wide with more bricks at the bottom and with supporting bricks as you build up, you can have a tower that is both strong and tall! You can think of prayer as a major source of strength and support as you build the tower of your life as a follower of Jesus. You want your life in Him to be strong and not easily toppled!

Spending time in God's Word, learning at a Bible-teaching church, serving God by serving others, and having fellowship with other Christians are good sources of strength and support for your life of following Jesus. If these are all part of your life now and continue as you grow up, just think how strong and tall for God you can be as a grown-up!

....

Dear God, I want to be built up strong in my faith in You. Help me to pray and learn and serve You all of my days! Amen.

Praise Is Powerful

Go into His gates giving thanks and into His holy place with praise. Give thanks to Him. Honor His name.
PSALM 100:4

When you take time to thank God for the things He has done in your life, it's powerful. Being grateful for who He is makes a difference in your heart. It builds trust and courage for what's ahead. Praise is a game changer because it shifts your attitude and your focus.

Think about it. How can you feel hopeless about your family situation when you're busy thanking God for all He is preparing to do? If you're focused on God's promise to never leave you, how can you feel alone? And being grateful for His strength gives you the freedom to trust He is working things out.

Take time today to thank God for being, well, God. Thank Him for having a perfect track record in your life, and tell God you're trusting Him now. Remind yourself of all the ways He's shown up and helped you with your friendships, fears, and insecurities. It helps you, and it will delight God!

. . . .

God, You're pretty amazing, and I am grateful You are in my life!

Day 301

Conversation Starters

*Is anyone among you suffering? He should pray.
Is anyone happy? He should sing songs of thanks to God.*
JAMES 5:13

Sometimes we play a little "High-Low" conversation game at bedtime where we share our best part of the day (the high) and our worst part of the day (the low). Sometimes we get a little carried away also sharing our most boring part and funniest part and stinkiest part and scariest part and on and on, until I realize Jodi and Lilly are really just trying to delay going to sleep. Ha!

But truly, it's so good to share about our days with each other. These conversation starters can also be great prayer starters. Invite God into every conversation, knowing He's already constantly present with you anyway and loves to be welcome. When you're sharing about the different events of the day and how they made you feel, give any worries and fears and needs to God and praise Him for all the good things. He cares about every high and every low and everything in between.

....

Dear God, please help me to remember Your constant presence with me. I welcome You into every part of my life, into every conversation. I love You and need You! Amen.

Day 302

Stepping In with Truth

So Manoah said to his wife, "We will die for sure. For we have seen God." But his wife said to him, "If the Lord had wanted to kill us, He would not have received a burnt gift and grain gift from us. He would not have shown us all these things, or let us hear these things."
JUDGES 13:22–23

Like many of us, Manoah was tempted to freak out in fear. God had just visited him, and he began to panic. Maybe he felt unworthy or maybe he was just plain scared. Either way he was certain he and his wife were about to take their last breath. But she confidently stepped in, pointing out truth that eventually calmed him down.

We all need people who can help us take a deep breath when we're scared. Who does that for you? Who are the ones who can calm you down? A friend or parent? A teacher or coach? An older brother or aunt? Are you that person for someone else? Let's find courage to speak up whenever others need to hear the truth.

....

God, help me to be known as a truth teller!

Day 303

Real Love

And now we have these three: faith and hope and love, but the greatest of these is love.
1 CORINTHIANS 13:13

Our world has a lot of wrong ideas about what love is, so we need God's instructions about love more than anything else! He *is* love, 1 John 4:8 tells us. All real love flows from Him and His Word. None of us would know anything about love if not for God!

First Corinthians 13 teaches us that real love "does not give up. Love is kind. Love is not jealous. Love does not put itself up as being important. Love has no pride. Love does not do the wrong thing. Love never thinks of itself. Love does not get angry. Love does not remember the suffering that comes from being hurt by someone. Love is not happy with sin. Love is happy with the truth. Love takes everything that comes without giving up. Love believes all things. Love hopes for all things. Love keeps on in all things. Love never comes to an end" (verses 4–8).

Dear God, help me to learn and live by what You say about real love—because You are real love! Amen.

Day 304

The Courage to Face Peer Pressure

So the Lord said, "I will destroy man whom I have made from the land, man and animals, things that move upon the earth and birds of the sky. For I am sorry that I have made them." But Noah found favor in the eyes of the Lord. This is the story of Noah and his family. Noah was right with God. He was without blame in his time. Noah walked with God.
GENESIS 6:7–9

Noah had the courage to be holy when everyone around him was not. Rather than sin to be like everybody else, Noah chose to do what he knew was right in God's eyes. Noah didn't give in to peer pressure. Instead, he decided to be righteous.

That kind of choice takes bravery. It's easy to follow others into bad decisions because we want to fit in. We want to be liked. We want to hang out with those girls. And rather than stand firm in what we know is right, we give in.

Courageous girl, choose to be like Noah. Choose to be right with God rather than doing the wrong things to fit in.

God, I choose You!

No Complaints

Do everything without complaining and arguing.
PHILIPPIANS 2:14 NLT

When I asked Jodi and Lilly to name their least favorite thing to do around the house, Jodi said sweeping the floor and Lilly said cleaning her room. I'm guessing you have some least favorite chores too. I know I sure do! It's easy to complain about them, but God's Word says not to complain about anything! And it really just makes the job all the worse to get done (and maybe even take longer, and who wants that?) if we choose a bad attitude while we work.

We sure don't do this perfectly, but we try to make cleanup time a time of praise and prayer. We can put on good worship music and sing while we do our chores. Then our minds focus on God and His love instead of grumpy thoughts wishing our houses would just clean themselves.

Ask God to help you make a habit of pushing negative, complaining thoughts out of your brain. If complaints never stay in your brain, they can never move to your mouth or spread into a really bad attitude.

. . . .

Dear God, I don't want to be a complainer. I need Your help all the time to replace complaining with good and positive thoughts, especially praise and worship to You! Amen.

Day 306

Taking the First Step

They carried it to the Jordan and put their feet in the water. (For the Jordan water floods during the time of gathering grain.) Then the water flowing down from above stood and rose up in one place far away at Adam, the city beside Zarethan. The water flowing down toward the sea of the Arabah, the Salt Sea, was all cut off. So the people crossed beside Jericho.
JOSHUA 3:15–16

Think of the bravery it took to step into the river when the waters were high and fast. The Israelites were trusting scared, believing God would stop the waters like He promised. . .and He did. The people crossed the Jordan River on dry ground.

Sometimes we have to take the first step before God shows up. We have to be the one to confront our friend or be honest with a parent. We have to say no to the party or yes to meeting with a tutor. God often asks that we trust Him enough to step out in faith. Where's God asking that of you right now?

God, I am afraid to move forward. Will You give me courage to take the next right step?

Day 307

Communication, Not Complaints

"If your brother sins against you, go and tell him what he did without other people hearing it."
MATTHEW 18:15

Sometimes people who just love to have everything peaceful can take a verse like Philippians 2:14, which says to do everything without complaining, a little too far. Does it mean don't complain if your friend wants you to give her your homework to copy? Of course not. There are absolutely many times to *not* do things but to stand up and say, "This is not okay."

Complaining should never be confused with communicating and working out conflict. We need to have hard conversations sometimes to help improve relationships and situations. For example, telling your sister you're frustrated with the unfair way she uses your stuff without asking is *not* complaining. You need to talk and work out the situation together, not just keep letting her get away with being selfish and disrespectful toward you. We should pray for God to help us embrace good communication and good conflict. Fear of constructive conflict is one of Satan's tactics to keep people sinning and trying to exert unfair power over each other rather than working toward good relationships and teamwork.

....

Dear God, help me to be wise and know the difference between complaining and good communication. I want to be able to work out conflict in good and healthy ways with Your help! Amen.

Facing the Bullies

As he talked with them, Goliath the Philistine from Gath came out of the army of the Philistines, and spoke the same words as before. And David heard him. When all the men of Israel saw the man, they ran away from him and were very much afraid.
1 SAMUEL 17:23–24

Goliath was a huge man, highly trained in combat. He had the best armor and was very strong. Goliath had a reputation of being a killing machine, and He wasn't afraid to brag about it. No one wanted to face that giant in battle.

We all have Goliaths in our life, those people who taunt us and make us feel small. Maybe it's the mean girls at school or the neighbor down the street. Maybe it's someone online or a teammate. It could even be someone in our own family who is quick to say mean and hurtful things.

God is not okay with anyone bullying you. If you ask, He'll give you strength to stand up for yourself, courage to not cower in fear, and confidence to know the truth about who you are.

....

God, help me to stand strong against the bullies. I need Your help.

Day 309

Be a God Pleaser

*I'm not trying to win the approval of people, but of God.
If pleasing people were my goal, I would not be Christ's servant.*
GALATIANS 1:10 NLT

To want approval means you want to be accepted and found pleasing and good. And it's hard not to want that from people when you desire to have friends and get along well with people. But God's Word shows us we shouldn't be looking for approval from people. We should look for God's approval most of all.

If you start praying now while you're young to be a God pleaser and a servant of Jesus, not a people pleaser, you'll help yourself out in so many ways! You won't be so worried what other people think of you. You won't want to give in to peer pressure. You'll be true to the unique, amazing person God designed you to be. You'll follow the awesome plan God has for you and have the most rewarding kind of life! You might not always get this right, because living for God's approval can be hard! But as you pray, God will help you keep your focus on Him, and at the same time He'll be filling your life with the good and loving relationships you need with others.

....

Dear God, I want to please You! I need Your help to keep my attention on what You think of me and want for me, not what others think and want. Please keep showing me how when my focus is on You, everything else in my life falls into place exactly like You want, and that is the very best life! Amen.

Day 310

Fearless Trust

But David said to Saul, "Your servant was taking care of his father's sheep. When a lion or a bear came and took a lamb from the flock, I went after him and fought him and saved it from his mouth. When he came against me, I took hold of him by the hair of his head and hit him and killed him. Your servant has killed both the lion and the bear. And this Philistine who has not gone through our religious act will be like one of them. For he has made fun of the armies of the living God." And David said, "The Lord Who saved me from the foot of the lion and from the foot of the bear, will save me from the hand of this Philistine." Saul said to David, "Go, and may the Lord be with you."
1 SAMUEL 17:34–37

David knew his courage came from God and that faith enabled him to fight Goliath.

Do you trust God will give you courage to face the hard days at school and home? If not, ask God for bold faith every day.

. . . .

God, help me to trust You fearlessly when I'm scared.

Real Girl Power

If Christ keeps giving me his power, I will gladly brag about how weak I am. Yes, I am glad to be weak or insulted or mistreated or to have troubles and sufferings, if it is for Christ. Because when I am weak, I am strong.
2 Corinthians 12:9–10 cev

There's a lot of talk about girl power in our world today, and it's good to want to be a strong girl. But sometimes our world's idea of strong girls is very different from God's will and His ways. To be truly strong, Jodi, Lilly, and I pray for God to help us be strong *in Him*. The Bible actually tells us to be happy about our weaknesses because when we can admit we are weak we can ask God for His power and He will keep giving it! On our own, we could never have greater power than God's, so being filled with God's limitless power is absolutely amazing! He loves to give it, so look at your weakness as a blessing, admit it, and then ask God to make you a mighty strong girl in His power!

Dear God, I admit my many weaknesses and I'm glad for them because they make me depend on You. Please fill me with Your awesome power and strength and make me a truly strong girl. Thank You! Amen.

Find Your Own Armor

Then Saul dressed David with his clothes. He put a brass head covering on his head, and dressed him with heavy battle-clothes. David put on his sword over his heavy battle-clothes and tried to walk, for he was not used to them. Then David said to Saul, "I cannot go with these, for I am not used to them." And David took them off.
1 Samuel 17:38–39

Just like King Saul was dressing David in his personal armor for battle, sometimes others want you to face giants like they did. Their hearts are in the right place. They love you and want to help, but their way may not be the right way for you. And that's okay.

What are you struggling with right now? Where's your battle? Is it at home? Are you fighting with friends? Are you feeling left out at school? Are insecurities keeping you from being yourself? Is someone being mean and hurting your feelings? Ask God to show you the armor He wants you to put on so you can face those challenges victoriously.

. . . .

God, I'm not sure how to handle hard situations. Will You show me what to do?

Day 313

Only One?

As He was going into one of the towns, ten men with a bad skin disease came to Him. They stood a little way off. They called to Him, "Jesus! Teacher! Take pity on us!" When Jesus saw them, He said, "Go and show yourselves to the religious leaders." As they went, they were healed. One of them turned back when he saw he was healed. He thanked God with a loud voice. He got down on his face at the feet of Jesus and thanked Him. He was from the country of Samaria. Jesus asked, "Were there not ten men who were healed? Where are the other nine? Is this stranger from another country the only one who turned back to give thanks to God?" Then Jesus said to him, "Get up and go on your way. Your trust in God has healed you."
Luke 17:12–19

Hopefully you've been learning since you were very small to be polite and always say please and thank you. But this account in Luke 17 reminds us how easy it is to forget to say thank you. These ten men had been miraculously healed by Jesus. You'd think they would have been brimming over with gratitude. Yet only one of them turned back to Jesus to actually thank and worship Him. In whatever ways God blesses us, we should always want to be like the one man and not the other nine!

Dear God, please help me never to forget to give You thanks for all You do for me! I want to worship and praise You for everything. Amen.

Day 314

Keeping It Simple

David put his hand into his bag, took out a stone and threw it, and hit the Philistine on his forehead. The stone went into his forehead, so that he fell on his face to the ground. So David won the fight against the Philistine with a sling and a stone. He hit the Philistine and killed him. There was no sword in David's hand.
1 SAMUEL 17:49–50

All it took to beat the ginormous giant was one stone. David didn't need shiny armor or a massive sword. He didn't need an army to assist him. He didn't train in kung fu or some other martial art. He simply battled the way he knew how: trusting God.

Finding courage to face the giant things in life comes from God alone. It's a simple truth that takes big faith. But that simple truth packs a powerful punch to the giants that threaten you. Ask God to fill you so full of faith that you can stand firm no matter what.

....

God, sometimes it's difficult to trust You in the hard times. Help me to remember the simple truth that You'll give me what I need to face challenges.

Day 315

Count Them Up

Sing in your heart to the Lord. Always give thanks for all things to God the Father in the name of our Lord Jesus Christ.
EPHESIANS 5:19-20

To help you be like the one man in Luke 17 and not the other nine, start now to make mental and/or written lists as a way to thank God regularly for your many blessings! Maybe you go around the table at Thanksgiving and do this with your family, but don't ever let it be a once-a-year kind of thing. Whether in your own personal prayers or with others, tell God constantly what you're thankful for. When you're focused more on blessings than on needs and worries, you'll find yourself filled with joy!

Maybe you've heard this old hymn by Johnson Oatman Jr. (or maybe not), but its words are timeless and needed still today and always!

Count your blessings, name them one by one;
Count your blessings, see what God has done;
Count your blessings, name them one by one,
And it will surprise you what the Lord has done.

....

Dear God, help me to focus on my blessings all the time. You have given me so many gifts and provided for me in so many ways, and I know You will continue. Thank You! Amen.

Day 316

Love Them Anyway

"I say to you who hear Me, love those who work against you. Do good to those who hate you."
LUKE 6:27

Sometimes the last thing you want to do is love others, especially when those others are nasty and mean. But God is asking you to love them anyway. He's asking you to treat them with respect even when they're treating you with hatred. And that's not easy to do!

God wants you to take care of yourself. You don't have to be a doormat that others walk on, but you can refuse to get down to their level. That means when they spread rumors about you, you don't have to spread rumors about them. When they call you names, you don't have to call them names. But you can talk to someone you trust and ask their advice. You can find safe adults to help you manage the situation.

You aren't loving them for their benefit but for yours. It keeps your heart from being bitter and cold, and it shows others that you're a Jesus girl.

God, I'm gonna need Your help with this! Give me the courage to love them anyway.

Prayer Calendar

We always pray and give thanks to God for you.
COLOSSIANS 1:3

Jodi loves to get on the computer and design documents using the features in Microsoft Word. Most programs like that have a calendar creator where you can choose a fun design and insert pictures and art for your own personal calendar. If you don't have access to that kind of computer program, you could simply get paper and pen and draw and design your own calendar. Once you have it designed and organized to match the year, fill it up with specific names of people to pray for: family members, friends, neighbors, teachers, instructors, coaches, pastors and church leaders and volunteers, missionaries, health care providers—the list goes on and on! You might be surprised how quickly you get to 365 names! And if not, you can start over and list names more than once. The point is, find creative ways to remember to pray for the specific people in your life. You can never pray for anyone too much!

Dear God, help me to think of creative ways to remember people in prayer. I'm grateful for all the people You have placed in my life, and we all need You! Amen.

Day 318

Out of Your Comfort Zone

Moses said to the Lord, "Lord, I am not a man of words. I have never been. Even now since You spoke to Your servant, I still am not. For I am slow in talking and it is difficult for me to speak." Then the Lord said to him, "Who has made man's mouth? Who makes a man not able to speak or hear? Who makes one blind or able to see? Is it not I, the Lord? So go now. And I will be with your mouth. I will teach you what to say." But Moses said, "O Lord, I ask of You, send some other person."
EXODUS 4:10–13

Sometimes doing what God is asking of you feels super scary. You worry you don't have what it takes or that it will make others dislike you. You may even question if you're actually hearing God's voice at all.

But God asks us to step out of comfort zones all the time, and He will equip us to obey. Ask for the courage to say yes!

....

God, give me courage to trust You as I say yes to what You're asking of me.

How Long?

I wait for the Lord. My soul waits and I hope in His Word.
PSALM 130:5

Sometimes it's really hard to be patient and wait on God's answers to prayer. In those times, we can find comfort in the fact that the prophet Habakkuk felt impatient too. He prayed, "O Lord, how long must I call for help before You will hear? I cry out to You, 'We are being hurt!' But You do not save us. Why do you make me see sins and wrong-doing? People are being destroyed in anger in front of me. There is arguing and fighting. The Law is not followed. What is right is never done. For the sinful are all around those who are right and good, so what is right looks like sin" (Habakkuk 1:2–4).

And we can learn from God's response that our human minds can never fully know and understand what God is doing in the times when it feels like He's taking much too long to answer our prayers: "Look among the nations, and see! Be surprised and full of wonder! For I am doing something in your days that you would not believe if you were told" (Habakkuk 1:5).

....

Dear God, help me to remember that You do things my mind can never fully understand. Help me to remember that just because I feel impatient doesn't mean You are not working out Your plans in exactly the right ways. You are good, and I trust You and hope in You. Amen.

Day 320

The Fear of Rejection

About three o'clock Jesus cried with a loud voice,
"My God, My God, why have You left Me alone?"
MATTHEW 27:46

We've all felt the pain of rejection. Few things hurt more than when your friends turn their backs on you or when you don't get the invite to the big birthday party. It stings when you don't get picked for the team or others talk behind your back. Unfortunately, rejection is something we will all face from time to time.

But how comforting to know that Jesus faced it too. That means He completely understands how bad it feels. He is able to relate when your feelings are hurt. So, courageous girl, you can talk to Jesus about it because He gets it.

Take a minute and tell Him how you're feeling. Let Him know where you're struggling and where you've been hurt. Tell Him your self-doubts. Ask Him to bring comfort and peace and to give you courage to love yourself.

....

God, I'm glad You understand how much rejection hurts. It makes me doubt my goodness. Please give me strength to know I am lovable.

Day 321

Creative Like Your Creator

The Lord is the everlasting God, the Creator of all the earth.
Isaiah 40:28 NLT

Have you ever tried to start a project for school that needed to be really creative but you just feel totally stuck? We get it. We've been there! In those frustrating times, remember whose you are! You are a child of the almighty Creator God. Remember that after God put earth, sky, water, sun, moon, and stars in place, He created every cool plant and animal and then people. Genesis 1:27 (NLT) says, "God created human beings in his own image. In the image of God he created them; male and female he created them." Never forget that you are made in His image!

Ask Him to help you with some fresh, new ideas and then keep thinking and working. You might be surprised when He answers by causing cool, creative ideas to pop into your brain!

....

Dear God, sometimes I feel like I can't think of any good ideas. Please help me when I'm stuck and frustrated. You designed me with a brain that is capable of so much. May I use it well and think and do like You want me to. I want to be creative like You, my amazing Creator! Amen.

Day 322

When God Builds, the Enemy Tries to Destroy

Those who were building the wall and those who carried loads did their work with one hand, and held something to fight with in the other hand. Each builder wore his sword at his side as he built.
NEHEMIAH 4:17–18

When Nehemiah and the others were rebuilding the wall around Jerusalem, the local people didn't want it to happen. They wanted the city to stay in ruins. But God had other plans and sent Nehemiah to secure the wall.

The truth is that whatever God builds, the Enemy tries to destroy. That's why we work with one hand and hold a weapon in the other. The best weapon available to us is the Bible. There's power in God's Word because it teaches us how to overcome the hard things we face. It encourages us when we feel down, and it reminds us of how much we're loved. It gives us courage.

When the devil tries to keep you down and discouraged, you can always find hope by reading the Bible. God will meet you there every time.

God, thank You for the Bible. Your Word is powerful!

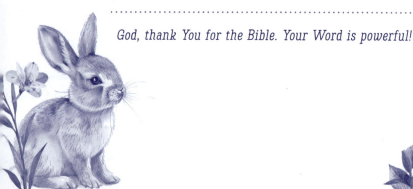

Love Covers

Most of all, have a true love for each other. Love covers many sins.
1 PETER 4:8

This scripture is one of our favorites. We're not proud of this, but Jodi and Lilly and I sometimes get angry and frustrated with each other and say and do things we later regret. Usually it's because we're not giving enough patience to each other or we're not listening well or we're letting selfishness take over. And so we find ourselves stopping to pray a lot: *God, please forgive us and help us forgive each other, and cover our mistakes with Your love and grace.* And once we pray like that, we can communicate better in peaceful ways and move forward trying to work out what's causing our conflict and unkind words and actions.

Something I remind Jodi and Lilly of all the time is that no matter what conflict we're going through, with God's help we will always work it out—because our love for each other is so great, and God's love for us is far, far greater. We never want sin to win at tearing apart our loving relationships.

....

Dear Jesus, thank You most of all for Your great love. You covered all our sin with Your blood when You took sin upon Yourself and died on the cross. You didn't deserve to die, but that's how much You love us! Wow! Help us to model Your great love and grace with each other. Amen.

Day 324

The Power to Save

"My God sent His angel and shut the lions' mouths. They have not hurt me, because He knows that I am not guilty, and because I have done nothing wrong to you, O king." Then the king was very pleased and had Daniel taken up out of the hole in the ground. So they took Daniel out of the hole and saw that he had not been hurt at all, because he had trusted in his God.
Daniel 6:22–23

Even all alone and surrounded by hungry lions, Daniel was saved from certain death. The cats thought their next meal was going to be an easy one, but it wasn't. An angel shut their mouths, and Daniel survived the night.

This story shows the mighty power of God to save us. He is the ultimate authority and His will, will be done. Even more, when we trust God with our situation, He will show up.

Where do you need God right now? Are you struggling in a relationship? Are you full of anger at something unfair? Find the courage to trust God sees you and will save you.

. . . .

God, I need You to save me!

Put Away and Pray

"If My people who are called by My name put away their pride and pray, and look for My face, and turn from their sinful ways, then I will hear from heaven. I will forgive their sin, and will heal their land."
2 Chronicles 7:14

This scripture is God's response to Solomon's prayer, but it is a response we today can learn from too. For God to answer our prayers, He wants us to put away our pride and pray, look for Him, and turn away from sin. Each time you are praying and needing God to listen and answer, you can think about this scripture and ask yourself, *Am I letting pride get in the way? Am I searching for God and His will? Do I have any sin in my life that I need to turn from and ask forgiveness for?*

Another scripture to remember is James 4:3: "Or if you do ask, you do not receive because your reasons for asking are wrong. You want these things only to please yourselves." And so you can ask yourself when you're praying, *Do I only want this to make myself happy?*

Dear God, I want to make You happy with my prayers because You are so awesome and You love me so much. I want to look for You more than I look for anything for myself. Please help me. Amen.

Day 326

Just Making Sure

Then Gideon said to God, "Do not let Your anger burn against me for speaking to You once again. Let me make one more test with the wool. Let it be dry only on the wool. And let the ground be wet all around it." God did so that night. For it was dry only on the wool. And all the ground was wet around it.
JUDGES 6:39–40

Gideon wanted to make double-sure he heard God right, so he boldly asked God to reconfirm the truth a second time. The Lord was gracious enough to meet Gideon's request.

This story reminds us that we can confidently ask God for clarity. We can ask Him to tell us again or in a different way. . .just to be sure. If you think God is asking you to do something, it's okay to double-check.

What's God asking that you need to confirm before moving forward? Is He opening or closing a door? Is His Holy Spirit giving you a gut-check about a decision? Be brave and ask God to verify, and He will.

. . . .

God, I'm just making sure that I've heard You right. Will You tell me again?

Day 327

Wake-Up Prayer

In the morning, O Lord, You will hear my voice. In the morning I will lay my prayers before You and will look up.
PSALM 5:3

Isn't it neat how God made some animals like owls and bats and skunks and hedgehogs want to stay up all night and sleep all day and others that are the opposite? I'm thankful He made people different this way too. What would we do if we didn't have some people willing to work all-night jobs, like in hospitals and fire stations? We should be so thankful for the differences in each person God created and how we can all work together!

Whatever time of day you love to wake up or simply have to wake up to get to school in time, start your day with prayer. Even before you get out of bed (or maybe you can roll out of bed and then kneel beside it!) ask God how you can best serve Him today, ask Him to bless you and keep you close to Him, ask Him to help you depend on His strength and power, ask Him to give you wisdom and teach you and guide you, and ask Him to help you share His love and truth with others.

....

Dear God, each day when I wake up, no matter what time, please help my thoughts go first to You! Show me how to serve You each day. Please bless me and help me to stay close to You. Please give me Your strength and power through Your Holy Spirit. Please give me wisdom and teach me and guide me, and help me to share Your truth and love with those around me. Amen.

Day 328

Simply Unshakable

Then Caleb told the people in front of Moses to be quiet. And he said, "Let us go up at once and take the land. For we are well able to take it in battle." But the men who had gone up with him said, "We are not able to go against the people. They are too strong for us."
NUMBERS 13:30–31

Caleb wasn't about to back down. He knew God had given them the land, so the size of the people there didn't worry him. He wasn't afraid of them because he trusted God and believed Him. Even when others in the scouting party felt afraid and overwhelmed, Caleb did not. His faith in God was simply unshakable.

It's easy to be afraid when you look at problems ahead. So often, they look too big or too scary, and you don't feel safe. Instead of trusting that God will help you, you check out. You quit. You give up. But what if you decided to have Caleb-like faith instead—the kind of faith where you knew God wouldn't let you fall? You'd be simply unshakable.

God, You're bigger than any problem I face. I believe it!

Day 329

Love and Discipline

"Don't make light of the Lord's discipline, and don't give up when he corrects you. For the Lord disciplines those he loves, and he punishes each one he accepts as his child."
HEBREWS 12:5–6 NLT

It can be really hard to think of discipline as something to love, so we need to pray for God's help with this! Do you feel like you always accept your parents' discipline with a good attitude? For example, let's say you have a regular chore of taking care of your dog, but then you continually forget to feed and walk the pup. As a consequence, you have to miss out on a fun event. In this scenario, do you gratefully thank your parents for what you're learning in the discipline process? Hmm. . .not easy, right? But it's because good parents want their children to learn good values and work ethic that they discipline their kids. It's because they love them. And God loves you more than the very best earthly parents, and He will discipline you to correct mistakes and to guide you. So start now while you're young, praying to accept and appreciate what God is doing when He disciplines you.

Dear God, remind me that You are always loving me perfectly, even if I don't always understand or enjoy exactly what You're doing. Please help me to appreciate that You correct and guide me with good discipline! Amen.

Day 330

More on Love and Discipline

As you endure this divine discipline, remember that God is treating you as his own children. Who ever heard of a child who is never disciplined by its father? If God doesn't discipline you as he does all of his children, it means that you are illegitimate and are not really his children at all. Since we respected our earthly fathers who disciplined us, shouldn't we submit even more to the discipline of the Father of our spirits, and live forever?
HEBREWS 12:7–9 NLT

Unfortunately these days, it's pretty easy to find parents who don't discipline their children much at all. This lack of discipline often shows up in awful and chaotic ways in these families' lives. I hope you can observe this kind of thing wisely and realize why discipline is good and loving. Hebrews 12 goes on to tell us why: "God's discipline is always good for us, so that we might share in his holiness. No discipline is enjoyable while it is happening—it's painful! But afterward there will be a peaceful harvest of right living for those who are trained in this way" (Hebrews 12:10–11 NLT).

Dear God, I want to share in Your holiness and I want the peaceful life that comes from being trained by discipline. So please remind me in the middle of discipline I don't enjoy that these are the things You're doing in my life. I am so grateful to be Your child! Amen.

Day 331

Even When Things Don't Make Sense

Then God said to Abraham, "As for Sarai your wife, do not call her name Sarai. But Sarah will be her name. And I will bring good to her. I will give you a son by her. I will bring good to her. And she will be the mother of nations. Kings of many people will come from her." Then Abraham fell on his face and laughed. He said to himself, "Will a child be born to a man who is 100 years old?"
GENESIS 17:15–17

Can you imagine laughing at God? Abraham was so caught off guard by this crazy promise of a child at his age that he couldn't help but fall down and giggle. But God is in the business of doing things that don't make sense.

What that means for you is that you can ask God for the big things. You can ask for things that seem absolutely impossible and unrealistic. Not only can He answer your prayer, but so often He does! Be bold and fearless in your requests, but at the same time, be prepared to trust His answers no matter what.

God, I'm believing You for big things!

Day 332

Obeying Even When You Don't Feel Like It

*Joseph awoke from his sleep. He did what the angel of
the Lord told him to do. He took Mary as his wife.*
MATTHEW 1:24

Joseph learned his soon-to-be wife, Mary, was pregnant. Because they weren't yet married, he knew the baby was not his. The angel's visit revealed that Mary was carrying baby Jesus. In faith, Joseph chose to obey God and take Mary as his wife. He may not have felt like it, but he had the courage to obey anyway.

Sometimes it takes everything you have to do as you're told. Your parents may have rules you think are silly, and your teacher may be stricter than she needs to be. Coaches and leaders may require things from you that feel confining. But these rules are in place to protect you.

As long as it doesn't hurt you emotionally or physically, there are benefits to obeying even when you don't feel like it. All throughout the Bible, God blesses those who obey. When you honor those in authority, God honors you as well.

*God, give me the courage to obey my
parents and other trusted adults.*

Endless Energy

Do not let yourselves get tired of doing good. If we do not give up, we will get what is coming to us at the right time. Because of this, we should do good to everyone. For sure, we should do good to those who belong to Christ.
GALATIANS 6:9–10

If we're not careful, it is really easy to get tired of doing good and making the right choices to obey God. Our enemy wants us to believe it's too hard and too exhausting to follow Jesus. Making bad choices and acting selfishly seems the easy, comfortable way a lot of the time. And sometimes it is a lot easier at first, but in the long run, God's ways are always best for us. And He will help us not to get worn out if we ask Him. He will help us get the good kind of rest we need (Matthew 11:28–30), and He will be the Bread of Life (John 6:32–59) and Living Water (John 4:1–15) that keep us going. He can give us the kind of endless energy we need for doing the good things He has planned for us, like doing good to others and sharing His love.

Dear God, help me to find everything I need in You so that I can keep doing good and never give up. Amen.

Sorta-Kinda Faith

Peter said to Jesus, "If it is You, Lord, tell me to come to You on the water." Jesus said, "Come!" Peter got out of the boat and walked on the water to Jesus. But when he saw the strong wind, he was afraid. He began to go down in the water. He cried out, "Lord, save me!" At once Jesus put out His hand and took hold of him. Jesus said to Peter, "You have so little faith! Why did you doubt?"
MATTHEW 14:28-31

Peter was all in. He was ready to step out of the boat and walk on water. But once he did—once he saw the waves and the wind—his faith sank. And so did he.

It's easy to have sorta-kinda faith, where we trust God until our situation gets hard or scary. The truth is that it takes courage to not doubt when the circumstances look doubtful. And sorta-kinda faith won't hold up when life get messy, because we'll take our eyes off Jesus.

Ask for courage to trust God no matter what.

....

God, make me brave so I don't have sorta-kinda faith. I don't ever want to doubt You!

Keep Going and Keep Growing

Do your best to add holy living to your faith. Then add to this a better understanding. As you have a better understanding, be able to say no when you need to. Do not give up. And as you wait and do not give up, live God-like. As you live God-like, be kind to Christian brothers and love them. If you have all these things and keep growing in them, they will keep you from being of no use and from having no fruit when it comes to knowing our Lord Jesus Christ.
2 PETER 1:5–8

Since Lilly was tiny, she has always loved to meet new people and make new friends. God has made her very social, loving to be around people and talk to them. She has found that a great way to use that gift is to reach out to people who look like they might be lonely.

You might be really social too, or you might be on the quieter side. Both are wonderful! What matters is that you're aware of how God made you to be and ask Him to use the personality and the gifts He's given you to serve Him the ways He asks. And He can continually grow and develop you with new traits and gifts and skills according to His will, so let Him! But to do these things the best, you need to stay in constant good relationship and communication with Him. So never stop praying. Never stop reading God's Word. Never stop learning from and serving your loving Father!

Dear God, help me to learn more about myself and how You designed me as I keep learning from You and staying close to You. Amen.

Day 336

Be a Bold Follower

The Lord turned and looked at Peter. He remembered the Lord had said, "Before a rooster crows, you will say three times that you do not know Me." Peter went outside and cried with a troubled heart.
LUKE 22:61–62

Right before Jesus looked at Peter, He'd been denied three times by him—just as Jesus told Peter he would. Peter was scared. It was a chaotic moment when his world was turned upside down. The man he chose to follow was being taken away, leaving Peter heartbroken and afraid. Rather than stand with courage, Peter hid.

It takes guts to stand up for what you believe. It may not be popular with your classmates or teammates. They may make fun of you for being a Jesus girl. They may even call you names for believing in God. What will you choose to do?

It's normal to be afraid to be bold in your faith. We all want to be liked, and we all want to fit in. But if you ask God for courage, He'll equip you to be a proud follower of His.

God, help me to be a bold follower of You!

Day 337

Take Care with Teasing

Put out of your life these things also: anger, bad temper, bad feelings toward others, talk that hurts people, speaking against God, and dirty talk.
COLOSSIANS 3:8

We love fun family movies, and we love to tease. So we often find ourselves teasing each other with funny quotes from our favorite movies. The 2018 *Peter Rabbit* movie is one of our more recent favorite movies with lots of laughs.

Even though silly teasing can be so funny and fun, we do have to be careful with it. We have to think of others' feelings and not take teasing so far that it actually becomes hurtful rather than fun. Ask God to help you have wisdom with this. He loves for us to laugh and be joyful. But He wants us to encourage and build each other up with our words, not tear anyone down with thoughtless teasing.

....

Dear God, thank You for fun and laughter and teasing that's silly and good. But please help me to be careful never to tease so much or so carelessly that it becomes hurtful to anyone. And if I do mess up with this, please help me to sincerely apologize and ask forgiveness quickly. And if others are teasing me too much and I'm being hurt, please help me to communicate my feelings well and work it out in healthy ways. Amen.

Day 338

Use Your Voice!

Moses asked the Lord what should be done. Then the Lord said to Moses, "The daughters of Zelophehad are right in what they say. Be sure to give them their own land among their father's brothers. Give them what would have been given to their father. And say to the people of Israel, 'If a man dies and has no son, then give what belongs to him to his daughter.'"
NUMBERS 27:5–8

Talk about bold! Back in the day, it was normal for the sons to inherit their father's land when he died, while daughters were left poor and penniless. But these five stood in front of Moses and pleaded their case, fearlessly asking for their dad's land since there were no brothers. Without God's intervention, Moses' approval, and their voices, they would've been left with nothing.

Be encouraged! Your voice matters! And you can fearlessly fight for what you know is right. You can speak up for yourself and others. And when you bring God into it, He'll give you determination to bring about change. With Him, you're a powerful force for good!

God, help me to stand up to things that need changing.

Day 339

Change of Plans

*The mind of a man plans his way,
but the Lord shows him what to do.*
PROVERBS 16:9

Has your family ever mapped out a great road trip, but then you came upon a closed highway and had to change your plans? Super frustrating! And you might never know what the problem was that closed the highway. You just know that police and safety officials who did know what was wrong closed it down. Maybe a car was on fire up ahead. Or maybe a sinkhole opened up. Yikes! (Lilly was pretty fascinated when she read a book about those recently!) Whatever the case, you made your plans and mapped out your route, but someone else changed them because they saw something you didn't and knew you would be better off not going the way you planned.

You can think of this example when you make your plans and then wonder why God doesn't help things turn out the way you thought they would or the way you worked toward. God sees and knows all, so far above and beyond what we can see. It's okay to make our plans (always asking for God's wisdom and direction as we do), but we need to work toward them while also giving them to God, praying like this:

. . . .

Dear God, I need Your wisdom and direction as I make plans. Please help them to honor You and follow Your will. I might not always understand the details, but I trust You are doing what is best and will make everything right someday. Amen.

If You Make a Promise, Keep It

Then she made a promise and said, "O Lord of All, be sure to look on the trouble of Your woman servant, and remember me. Do not forget Your woman servant, but give me a son. If You will, then I will give him to the Lord all his life. And no hair will ever be cut from his head."
1 SAMUEL 1:11

Hannah wanted a baby so badly, she could barely stand it, so she asked the Lord for a son, promising he'd spend his life serving God. Because He loved her so, God gave her a child she named Samuel. Because Hannah loved the Lord, she kept her promise and took him to the temple to be raised.

Promises are a big deal because you're giving your word that something will or will not happen. You are making an agreement. You're guaranteeing. Be sure that if you are bold enough to make a promise, you follow through with it. It's how you grow trust with your friends and family.

God, I want to be trustworthy. Help me to be the kind of girl who keeps her word.

God with You, Holding You

"Do not fear, for I am with you. Do not be afraid, for I am your God. I will give you strength, and for sure I will help you. Yes, I will hold you up with My right hand that is right and good."
ISAIAH 41:10

We learned the absolute truth of this scripture when we went through the hardest and most confusing time we've ever known—the unexpected death of a very dear loved one. Jodi and Lilly were totally heartbroken to lose their nana, just as I was to lose my mom. But as we look back now, we see how God never left us, for sure was our Strength, and absolutely held us up and carried us when we couldn't keep going on our own. He provided love and care in so many ways and through so many people, and He still does when we feel again the grief of losing and missing her.

We still don't understand why things had to happen the way they did, but we trust God anyway. We have seen His goodness and care firsthand and have felt Him so close during our worst pain. We will continue to trust Him. Isaiah 41:10 is a wonderful scripture to memorize and remember as you pray to the one true God who is your Strength and Help in any situation!

....

Dear God, please help me not to fear anything and to trust in Your strength no matter what. You have made me strong and carried me in the past, and I know You will continue to hold me up through any hard thing. Amen.

Day 342

The Courage to Ask for Change

The woman left her water jar and went into the town. She said to the men, "Come and see a Man Who told me everything I ever did! Can this be the Christ?" They went out of town and came to Him.
JOHN 4:28-30

This woman at the well was disliked. She'd made many bad choices that resulted in her being an outcast. But when she ran into town and spoke, she got their attention. No matter the sinful life she had lived, Jesus used her to bring others to Him.

Are you ashamed of some choices you've made? Are you afraid people won't listen to you anymore because you've screwed up? Maybe you cheated on a test or gossiped about a friend. Maybe you have been a mean girl or have been disobeying your parents. If so, let this story encourage you.

Spend some time confessing your sins to God and telling Him you want to be changed just like the woman at the well. Ask Him to let you be a light for your friends and family.

God, I'm boldly asking You to change my heart to love You and others more.

Day 343

God All-Powerful

Those who go to God Most High for safety will be protected by God All-Powerful.
PSALM 91:1 ICB

You might hear some of the news on television or read it online or in the paper or talk about it at school, and it might scare you with stories about fighting and wars and sicknesses and crime. But never forget who your God is—the all-powerful one! This scripture in Psalm 91 continues:

> I will say to the Lord, "You are my place of safety and protection. You are my God, and I trust you." God will save you from hidden traps and from deadly diseases. He will protect you like a bird spreading its wings over its young. His truth will be like your armor and shield. You will not fear any danger by night or an arrow during the day. You will not be afraid of diseases that come in the dark or sickness that strikes at noon. (Psalm 91:2–6 ICB)

There is such power in knowing and praying God's Word when you feel overcome with fear about things you cannot control. Remember that God *can* control all of it, and He loves you like crazy. Keep trusting in His love and talking to Him about everything!

Dear God, this world is super scary sometimes. I need You to remind me how much bigger You are than any bad thing, and how You love and protect me. I come to You for safety and peace, God. I love and trust You! Amen.

Day 344

The Courage to Lead

Now Lappidoth's wife Deborah, a woman who spoke for God, was judging Israel at that time. . . . She sent for Barak the son of Abinoam from Kedeshnaphtali, and said to him, "The Lord, the God of Israel, says, 'Go to Mount Tabor. Take with you 10,000 men from the sons of Naphtali and Zebulun. . . .'" Then Barak said to her, "I will go if you go with me. But if you do not go with me, I will not go."
JUDGES 4:4, 6, 8

Deborah was respected in a time when women weren't valued for their wisdom, courage, or leadership skills. She served as a prophet and judge to Israel, and both men and women looked to her for guidance. Even Barak, an army general, wouldn't go into battle without Deborah by his side. What a great example of girl power!

Deborah said yes when God put her in a leadership position. She may not have had all the answers, but Deborah knew God did. She trusted Him and allowed Him to use her in mighty ways. Where is God calling you to lead?

....

God, give me the courage to be a leader in my school and my community!

Day 345

Pray to Be Salt and Light

"You are the salt of the earth. If salt loses its taste, how can it be made to taste like salt again? It is no good. It is thrown away and people walk on it. You are the light of the world. You cannot hide a city that is on a mountain. Men do not light a lamp and put it under a basket. They put it on a table so it gives light to all in the house. Let your light shine in front of men. Then they will see the good things you do and will honor your Father Who is in heaven."
MATTHEW 5:13–16

Maybe at your school or in your activities you feel like it's a lot easier to just stay quiet about your faith in Jesus. But that's exactly what our enemy Satan wants you to think. Jesus tells us in the Bible we should want to be like salt and light. Salt helps food taste its best, and we should want to bring out the best in others and help show them life at its best. Life at its best is a life that believes in and follows Jesus.

Jesus also wants us to be the light of the world, helping show others the way to Him. If we hide our light, we can't help others see the way to Jesus. But if we shine our lights, giving Him honor through every good thing we do, we help others honor Him too.

....

Dear God, help me never to hide or be selfish with my faith in You. I want to reach out to others and be salt and light to them, helping them know and love You too! Amen.

Day 346

The Courage to Ask for More

When she came to Othniel, she talked him into asking her father for a field. When she got down off her donkey, Caleb said to her, "What do you want?" Achsah answered, "Give me a gift. You have given me the land of the Negev. Give me wells of water also." So Caleb gave her the wells in the high-land and in the valley.
JOSHUA 15:18–19

Caleb's daughter had courage to ask for more. Achsah was confident enough to step out in faith and push the limits, and it worked in her favor.

Do you ever settle for something rather than ask for more? Maybe you want a deeper friendship or more friends. Maybe you want to be on a different team or move from band to choir. Maybe you'd like to be class president rather than secretary. And rather than speak up for yourself, you allow insecurities to shut you down. If you don't ask, it may never change.

Tell God your heart's desire, and then boldly ask Him for what you really want.

....

God, it's scary to be brave. Will You give me the confidence to step out?

Day 347

The Shepherd's Leading

The Lord is my Shepherd.
PSALM 23:1

If you're ever feeling stressed and anxious about anything at all, Psalm 23 offers such beautiful comfort and peace to focus on as you pray. God is your loving shepherd, but if you're not following Him, where will you end up? But if you do let Him guide you all your life, you will find everything you need plus peace and joy no matter your circumstances.

Psalm 23 continues:

> I will have everything I need. He lets me rest in fields of green grass. He leads me beside the quiet waters. He makes me strong again. He leads me in the way of living right with Himself which brings honor to His name. Yes, even if I walk through the valley of the shadow of death, I will not be afraid of anything, because You are with me. You have a walking stick with which to guide and one with which to help. These comfort me. You are making a table of food ready for me in front of those who hate me. You have poured oil on my head. I have everything I need. For sure, You will give me goodness and loving-kindness all the days of my life. Then I will live with You in Your house forever. (Psalm 23:1–6)

Dear Lord, thank You for being my good shepherd and providing everything I need. You calm my heart as I trust and follow You! Amen.

Day 348

Overcoming Fear with Faith

Then Mary said, "I am willing to be used of the Lord. Let it happen to me as you have said." Then the angel went away from her.
LUKE 1:38

The angel Gabriel had just told Mary she was going to be pregnant with Jesus. Rather than run away scared or say no, she said, "I am willing." Can you even imagine how scared she must have been? She was going to grow a big baby belly for all to see, and she wasn't even married. She must have worried what others would think or if anyone would believe that God planted the baby inside her. What a scary situation!

But Mary trusted even though she was afraid. She submitted to God's plans for her, and she decided that fear would not get the best of her. She chose faith instead.

Where is God asking you to trust Him rather than give in to worry? What's keeping you from it?

....

God, sometimes what You ask of me is scary. Make me brave so my faith is bigger than my fear.

Day 349

Love Your Leaders

Remember your leaders who first spoke God's Word to you. Think of how they lived, and trust God as they did.
HEBREWS 13:7

If you're keeping a prayer journal, a great idea is to think of and list all the people who have helped and are still helping lead you in your faith. Maybe your parents or grandparents or your pastor or Sunday school teacher or VBS leader. Maybe all of the above! Thank God for these specific people and how they helped you to know God and follow Jesus. Ask Him to bless them. If you know some of their specific needs, talk to God about those. Pray for God to bring them great encouragers and ask Him how you can encourage them.

Probably the best way to encourage them is to continue to live your life in obedience to God's Word as they continue to as well. God-loving leaders are rewarded richly when they are able to watch those they helped continue to follow God and do the good things He has planned.

Mostly, pray for Christian leaders to continue to be strong in their faith, no matter what life brings their way, and to be leaders to others in addition to you!

....

Dear God, thank You for the awesome people who have helped me to know and love You and who keep on doing that! I am so grateful for them. Please bless and help them in everything. Help us to encourage each other as we live for You! Amen.

Course Correction

The angel of the Lord found Hagar by a well of water in the desert on the way to Shur. He said, "Hagar, you who serve Sarai, where have you come from and where are you going?" And she said, "I am running away from Sarai, the one I serve." Then the angel of the Lord said to her, "Return to your boss. Put yourself under her power."
Genesis 16:7–9

Going back to serve under Sarai was the last thing Hagar wanted to do. It wasn't comfortable, and she wanted out. She didn't want to stay with that family one more second. But that's exactly where God wanted her because He had a plan.

Sometimes God asks us to do things we don't understand. We think we have a better way. Rather than trust God has an awesome outcome in the works, we go our own way. But God has a reputation for correcting our course when we make the wrong turn.

Think about it. Is God asking you to go one way but you're going the opposite direction? What would it look like to trust Him?

God, give me the guts to follow You!

Pointing to Jesus

"You are to love each other. You must love each other as I have loved you. If you love each other, all men will know you are My followers."
JOHN 13:34–35

Jodi loves learning ballet, and when she's not in class, she's often dancing around our house or through a store as we're shopping. Her friend Leah told her recently, "You always stand in a ballet position," and they laughed together about it because it's often true. . .and Jodi hadn't really noticed! It just comes naturally now because she does ballet so often.

In a similar way, if we call ourselves followers of Jesus, others should often see us doing what Jesus says. If we've accepted Jesus as Savior and we're regularly spending time in God's Word and learning at church, then we should be doing what Jesus taught in the Bible and others should notice. We should be known for loving God first and loving others as ourselves. We should be known for being generous and helping take care of the needy. We should be known as praying people. We should be known as people who share God's truth and encourage others. We should be known as honest and fair and kind. We should never pretend to be perfect people, but we should point others to the only one who is perfect: Jesus Christ.

Dear God, I don't want to be fake or a show-off, but I humbly want others to notice that I love You and I follow Jesus. I know I can't follow You perfectly, but with Your help I can do my very best. Thank You! Amen.

Day 352

Pass It On

I remember your true faith. It is the same faith your grandmother Lois had and your mother Eunice had. I am sure you have that same faith also.
2 TIMOTHY 1:5

Timothy's faith was passed down to him through his mother and grandmother. Their family obviously had a long line of faithful women who benefited so many. Not only was it a family blessing back then, but Timothy is known as a pillar—an important person—in the faith and continues to encourage us even today.

Make a decision right now to pass your faith on to those around you. Choose to make a difference by living a life of faith and trust, and find the courage to make the hard choices that will encourage others to do the same. Be the kind of girl whose life points to God in heaven.

What lifestyle changes need to happen? Ask God for the courage it will take to be all in with your faith and for the determination it will take to walk it out. With His help, you can do it!

God, let me be the reason my friends and family know You. I want to make a difference!

Day 353

The God Who Answers by Fire: Part 1

Then the woman said to Elijah, "Now I know that you are a man of God. Now I know that the word of the Lord in your mouth is truth."
1 Kings 17:24

There is so much to learn from the prophet Elijah and the work and miracles God did through him. His showdown with the prophets of the false god Baal is an extraordinary true story of the Bible. He told the people of Israel to come together at Mount Carmel and asked them,

> "How long will you be divided between two ways of thinking? If the Lord is God, follow Him. But if Baal is God, then follow him." But the people did not answer him a word. Then Elijah said to the people, "I am the only man left who speaks for God. But here are 450 men who speak for Baal. Bring two bulls to us. Let them choose one bull for themselves and cut it up and put it on the wood. But put no fire under it. I will make the other bull ready and lay it on the wood. And I will put no fire under it. Then you call on the name of your god, and I will call on the name of the Lord. The God Who answers by fire, He is God." All the people answered and said, "That is a good idea." (1 Kings 18:21–24)

Dear God, just as Elijah was known as a man of Yours, I want to be known as a girl of Yours, and as someone who shares truth from You. I want to help show others that You are the one true God! Amen.

Day 354

The God Who Answers by Fire: Part 2

"The Lord, He is God. The Lord, He is God."
1 KINGS 18:39

The false god Baal had no answer for the people. So. . .

Elijah said to all the people, "Come near to me." So all the people came near to him. And he built again the altar of the Lord which had been torn down. . . . Then he set the wood in place. . . . The water flowed around the altar, and filled the ditch also. Then the time came for giving the evening gift. Elijah the man who spoke for God came near and said, "O Lord, God of Abraham, Isaac and Israel, let it be known today that You are God in Israel. Let it be known that I am Your servant, and have done all these things at Your word. Answer me, O Lord. Answer me so these people may know that You, O Lord, are God. Turn their hearts to You again." Then the fire of the Lord fell. It burned up the burnt gift, the wood, the stones and the dust. And it picked up the water that was in the ditch. All the people fell on their faces when they saw it. They said, "The Lord, He is God. The Lord, He is God." (1 Kings 18:30, 33, 35–39)

What an incredible story! I hope it gives you goose bumps!

Dear God, You are the one true God and I am Your servant. I want any good thing I do to bring praise to You and help others know You as God and Savior! Amen.

Day 355

The God Who Whispers Too

"What are you doing here, Elijah?"
1 KINGS 19:9

After the showdown, Elijah was on the run for his life. Discouraged and alone, he had a conversation with God:

> Elijah said, "I have been very careful to serve the Lord, the God of All. For the people of Israel have turned away from Your agreement. They have torn down Your altars and have killed with the sword the men who speak for You. Only I am left, and they want to kill me." So the angel said, "Go and stand on the mountain before the Lord." And the Lord passed by. A strong wind tore through the mountains and broke the rocks in pieces before the Lord. But the Lord was not in the wind. After the wind the earth shook. But the Lord was not in the shaking of the earth. After the earth shook, a fire came. But the Lord was not in the fire. And after the fire came a sound of gentle blowing. When Elijah heard it, he put his coat over his face, and went out and stood at the opening of the hole. Then a voice came to him and said, "What are you doing here, Elijah?" (1 Kings 19:10–13)

Other versions of the Bible call the gentle blowing a whisper, and once Elijah heard from God through that whisper, he continued on with the plans God had for him!

....

Dear God, help me to remember that You can speak to me in big, dramatic ways and sometimes in quiet ways like a whisper. I always want to be listening for You and obeying You! Amen.

Day 356

Courageous Choices

A woman came with a jar of perfume. She had given much money for this. As Jesus ate, she poured the perfume on His head. When the followers saw it, they were angry. They said, "Why was this wasted? This perfume could have been sold for much money and given to poor people." Jesus knew what they were saying. He said to them, "Why are you giving this woman trouble? She has done a good thing to Me."
MATTHEW 26:7–10

Sometimes the things you do for God don't make sense to the world. Choosing His way is often very different than going along with the crowd. And because you're deciding to live differently, others may make fun of you for it. They may call you lame or say you're a prude. They may criticize you and joke about your faith. What will you do if that happens?

Just like the woman pouring her expensive perfume on Jesus' feet, your decisions may be questioned. But God will see every courageous choice and will bless you for it.

God, give me courage to not care what others think of my faith. Help me to choose You every time.

Day 357

The Real Deal

Then Jesus said, "Someone touched Me because I know power has gone from Me." When the woman saw she could not hide it, she came shaking. She got down before Jesus. Then she told Jesus in front of all the people why she had touched Him. She told how she was healed at once. Jesus said to her, "Daughter, your faith has healed you. Go in peace."
Luke 8:46–48

This woman was so sick, and she had been for twelve years. She'd spent all her hope and money on doctors who couldn't fix her, and she was at the end of her rope. When she heard Jesus was passing through, she laced up her sandals and headed out to find Him. She had enough faith to believe Jesus was the answer. She touched His coat and was instantly healed.

Jesus is the real deal. He isn't some cute storybook character who magically makes things happen. He isn't a made-up person for weak people to believe in. Jesus is real. He is alive. And He is always available when you need help and healing.

Confidently reach out today and tell Him what you need.

....

God, I believe in You.

The Courage to Confess

The snake said to the woman, "No, you for sure will not die! For God knows that when you eat from it, your eyes will be opened and you will be like God, knowing good and bad." The woman saw that the tree was good for food, and pleasing to the eyes, and could fill the desire of making one wise. So she took of its fruit and ate. She also gave some to her husband, and he ate.
GENESIS 3:4–6

We will make colossal mistakes in our lifetime. We will believe the wrong thing or trust the wrong people. We will choose what we think is right and will learn it wasn't. And we'll even face decisions we know are wrong and disobediently say yes anyway. Yep, we will royally mess up!

But that's not the end of the story. Because of Jesus, you can confess those bad choices and be forgiven. It will take courage and humility to admit your failures, but God isn't expecting perfection from you. He loves you, and nothing can ever change that.

....

God, thank You for not expecting perfection. I confess that I make mistakes. Thanks for forgiveness!

Day 359

Stay in the Light

God is light. There is no darkness in Him. If we say we are joined together with Him but live in darkness, we are telling a lie. We are not living the truth. If we live in the light as He is in the light, we share what we have in God with each other.
1 JOHN 1:5–7

Which sounds better to you? Living somewhere dark and dirty or light and clean? Sin makes us stay dirty in darkness, but confessing (telling our sins to God) makes us clean and in the light again. No mistake or bad choice you make can ever cause God to love you less. He loves us always, no matter what. And He wants us to admit our sins to Him so He can wipe them away and help us live in the light and be a light to others.

Dear God, I want to live in Your light and be clean from my sin. Help me to stay away from the darkness and dirtiness of sin. I confess these sins to You today: _____. Please forgive me. I know You love me and will take them away from me. Thank You! Amen.

Day 360

God Is the Promise Keeper

Then the Lord visited Sarah as He had said and did for her as He had promised. Sarah was able to have a child and she gave birth to a son when Abraham was very old. He was born at the time the Lord said it would happen.
GENESIS 21:1–2

God made a promise to Abraham. He promised a son to him and his aging wife, Sarah. And at the ripe old age of one hundred, he became a father. The seemingly impossible promise came to pass, and Isaac was born.

Trusting for something that seemed so out of the question took a whole lot of faith. It would have been easier to not believe. Who wants to hope for something that probably won't happen? But God is in the business of the impossible. He is the ultimate promise keeper, which means you need to be in the business of fearless faith.

What are you trusting God for right now that feels hopeless? How can you strengthen your faith to believe?

....

God, help me to hold on to Your promises even when they feel impossible.

Day 361

Peacemaker

God blesses those people who make peace.
MATTHEW 5:9 CEV

We think all the "No Drama Llama" stuff you see in stores these days is pretty cute! Because unless it's the kind of drama like watching a play or a musical, or maybe a close competition like an exciting basketball game down to the last second, drama just for the sake of drama is not cool. We shouldn't love being in conflict and competition with others; instead, we should always want good and peaceful relationships, forgiving each other and not gossiping or causing fights.

Yet the Bible says blessed are the peace*makers*, and you can't *make* anything without some work, right? So it takes some working out of disagreements and trouble to make peace sometimes, not just going along with anything to try to keep everyone happy and drama-free. We need so much help and wisdom from God to know how to do this right. Fortunately, God promises us that He loves to give us wisdom (James 1:5). He totally loves to help us with our problems, so just keep asking!

....

Dear God, help me to be not only a no-drama llama but someone willing to work out conflict and be a peacemaker. I am so grateful for Your wisdom and help. I need You so much! Amen.

The Pressure to Be Beautiful

Jacob loved Rachel. So he said, "I will serve you seven years for your younger daughter Rachel." Laban said, "It is better that I give her to you than to another man. Stay with me." So Jacob worked seven years for Rachel. It was only like a few days to him, because of his love for her.
GENESIS 29:18–20

Jacob fell in love with Rachel and asked her father to let them marry. Laban agreed as long as Jacob worked for him the next seven years. So he did. But Laban tricked Jacob, and he unknowingly married Leah, the oldest daughter. She wasn't as pretty as Rachel, so Jacob agreed to work another seven years for Rachel's hand. And while it's okay that Jacob fell in love with one sister and not the other, it must have been hurtful to Leah.

There's a whole lot of pressure to be beautiful. And it's often an impossible standard to reach, much less maintain. It can leave you feeling unlovable. But you are your own kind of beautiful. Be brave enough to embrace it.

God, I am beautiful in my own way. Give me the courage to believe it.

Day 363

Trusting God in the Crazy

*So the people called out and the religious leaders blew
the horns. When the people heard the sound of the horns,
they called out even louder. And the wall fell to the ground.
All the people went straight in and took the city.*
JOSHUA 6:20

The battle plan God downloaded to Joshua to take the city of Jericho was crazy by most standards. It involved walking in circles, blowing horns, and screaming. Rather than usual weapons like swords, arrows, and knives, the Israelites' weapon was obedience. The city would be theirs if they obeyed.

God doesn't think like we do. His ways are not our ways. And sometimes what He's asking sounds absolutely crazy. But find the courage to obey anyway. Choose to trust God in the crazy.

What's God asking of you that seems unusual or silly? Is He asking you to befriend the new kid or try a new sport? Is He asking you to step out of a group or spend more time volunteering? Be brave and say yes to God. Then watch what happens next!

. . . .

God, I don't always understand You, but I will always trust You.

Day 364

Time to Let Go

She was going to have a baby, and she gave birth to a son. When she saw that he was beautiful, she hid him for three months. But the time came when she could hide him no longer. So she took a basket made from grass, and covered it with tar and put the child in it. And she set it in the grass by the side of the Nile.
EXODUS 2:2–3

The baby is Moses, and his mother was Jochebed. The pharaoh in Egypt was paranoid the Hebrew slaves were going to outnumber his people, so he ordered their newborns to be killed. Jochebed kept Moses hidden until she couldn't hide him anymore. And when the time came, she put together a plan to save his life. That courageous act allowed Moses to then go on to save the lives of millions.

There are times God calls us to let go of people we care about because He has different plans. It might be a friendship, a team, or someone else. Ask God to show you His will so you can stay in it.

God, give me courage to trust You.

Day 365

Asking in His Name

"Whatever you ask in My name, I will do it so the shining-greatness of the Father may be seen in the Son."
JOHN 14:13

Here we are ending this book on how God can grow you as a praying girl, and the end makes us think of how prayers often end with "In Jesus' name" and then "Amen." The words of John 14:13 are the reason we often say, "In Jesus's name." Every time we pray, we should want any answer to our prayer to bring shining-greatness, or glory and praise, to God!

And *amen* is a Hebrew word meaning "truly" or "so be it" that the writers of the Bible used; we model our prayers after them when we use *amen* today. It's just a way to end our prayers with the petition, *Please let what we've asked be true.*

As this book comes to a close, we want you to know we have been praying for you as you've read these devotionals. We hope you've learned a lot and had some fun reading too. We sure have!

Dear God, please bless each person reading this. Let us grow closer to You through prayer. Please guide and protect us and fill us with so much joy in knowing You, no matter what we are going through. Help us always to stay close to You as we learn from You and live for You because of Jesus our Savior. Amen

Scripture Index

OLD TESTAMENT

GENESIS
1:26–27 ....Day 120
3:4–6 .... Day 358
6:7–9 .... Day 304
16:7–9 .... Day 350
16:13 .... Day 222
17:15–17 ....Day 331
21:1–2.................... Day 360
28:15..................... Day 234
29:18–20 .... Day 362
50:20.................... Day 270

EXODUS
2:2–3 .... Day 364
4:10–13...................Day 318
20:11 .... Day 59
20:12 ....Day 125
33:11 ....Day 201
33:14....................... Day 74

NUMBERS
13:30–31................ Day 328
27:5–8................... Day 338

DEUTERONOMY
29:29.....................Day 166
31:6 .... Introduction

JOSHUA
1:5 .... Day 204
1:9 .... Day 1
3:15 16................... Day 306
6:20...................... Day 363
10:12–14 .... Day 279

15:18–19.................. Day 346

JUDGES
4:4, 6, 8.................. Day 344
6:39–40 .... Day 326
13:22–23 .... Day 302

1 SAMUEL
1:11......................... Day 340
16:7.................... Days 61, 76
17:23–24 .... Day 308
17:34–37..................Day 310
17:38–39..................Day 312
17:49–50 ....Day 314

1 KINGS
3:5..........................Day 189
3:10 ....Day 190
17:24...................... Day 353
18:39...................... Day 354
19:9 .... Day 355

2 KINGS
19:19 ....Day 163

1 CHRONICLES
16:11...............Days 186, 193
28:20.......................Day 42

2 CHRONICLES
7:14........................ Day 325

NEHEMIAH
4:17–18.................. Day 322
8:6......................... Day 275

ESTHER
4:16 .... Day 40

JOB
1:1 .... Day 257
12:7-10 .... Day 89
22:21 .... Day 290
40:2 .... Day 258

PSALMS
5:3 .... Day 327
8:1, 3-4 .... Day 281
18:29 .... Day 130
18:30 .... Day 192
18:32 .... Day 138
23:1 .... Day 347
23:2-3 .... Day 230
23:4 .... Day 272
25:4-5 .... Day 75
27:14 .... Days 3, 79
29:11 .... Day 280
30:2 .... Day 247
31:15-16 .... Day 256
31:18 .... Day 259
31:24 .... Day 7
32:8 .... Day 168
34:4 .... Day 30
34:8 .... Day 220
34:14-16 .... Day 101
34:17-18 .... Day 52
34:18 .... Day 153
37:4 .... Day 144
37:7 .... Day 121
37:23-24 .... Day 191
40:1-2 .... Day 238
46:1-3 .... Days 58, 291
46:5 .... Day 119
46:10 .... Days 19, 70, 268
52:8 .... Day 100
56:3-4 .... Day 66
56:8 .... Days 22, 153
61:2-4 .... Day 250
66:16-20 .... Day 63
73:23-24 .... Day 110
77:1 .... Day 283
77:11-12 .... Day 15
89:15 ....ay 210
91:1 .... Day 343
91:11-12 .... Day 128
94:22 .... Day 56
95:1-7 .... Day 233
100:4 .... Day 300
112:7 .... Day 114
118:5 .... Day 175
118:6-9 .... Day 175
118:24 .... Days 80, 253
119:9-11 .... Day 27
119:15-18 .... Day 235
119:105 .... Days 25, 174
119:165-167 .... Day 31
130:5 .... Days 88, 319
138:3 .... Day 36
139:1-4 .... Day 116
139:7-10 .... Day 50
145:1 .... Day 47
145:3-6 .... Day 286
145:17-21 .... Day 273
147:3 .... Day 153

Proverbs
1:7	Day 77
3:5-6	Day 102
4:23	Day 277
10:19	Day 118
11:2	Day 229
16:9	Day 339
17:22	Day 200
19:17	Day 219
19:21	Day 262
29:23	Day 225
29:25	Day 264

Ecclesiastes
3:1	Day 218
4:9-10	Day 215

Isaiah
9:6	Day 211
12:2	Day 140
26:3	Day 124
40:28	Day 321
40:31	Day 217
41:6	Day 18
41:10	Days 252, 341
41:13	Day 148
43:1	Day 5
43:2	Day 20
43:19	Day 208
55:9	Day 98
61:10	Day 172
64:8	Day 232

Jeremiah
17:7-8	Day 236
17:14	Day 159
29:11	Day 48
29:13	Day 96

Lamentations
3:24-26	Day 214

Daniel
3:12	Day 181
3:13-15	Day 292
3:17-18	Day 294
3:23	Day 182
6:10	Day 179
6:22-23	Day 324

Jonah
1:17	Day 245

Micah
7:7	Day 274

Habakkuk
3:17-18	Day 154
3:19	Day 94

Zephaniah
3:17	Day 152

Haggai
2:4	Day 16

Zechariah
2:13	Day 228

Malachi
3:10	Day 249

NEW TESTAMENT

Matthew
1:24	Day 332
5:9	Day 361
5:13–16	Day 345
5:43–48	Day 95
6:5–6	Day 69
6:8	Day 67
6:9	Day 21
6:20–21	Day 68
6:25	Day 85
6:34	Day 127
7:7	Day 199
8:8	Day 207
8:23–25	Day 187
11:28–30	Day 86
14:28–31	Day 334
14:29–30	Day 84
18:15	Day 307
18:20	Day 99
25:35–40	Day 57
26:7–10	Day 356
26:41	Day 83
27:46	Day 320
28:5–7	Day 150

Mark
9:24	Day 43
11:25–26	Day 65

Luke
1:30–31	Day 135
1:37	Day 64
1:38	Day 348
2:36–38	Day 265
6:27	Day 316
6:37	Day 170
6:38	Day 203
7:21–23	Day 105
8:5–8	Day 173
8:46–48	Day 357
10:41–42	Day 142
11:5–10	Day 71
11:11–13	Day 263
12:22–23	Day 298
12:25–26	Day 183
17:12–19	Day 313
18:1	Day 87
18:10–14	Day 223
22:61–62	Day 336

John
4:28–30	Day 342
6:5–10	Day 91
6:11–14	Day 92
6:32–35	Day 271
8:12	Day 282
10:4	Day 180
10:10	Day 266
13:34–35	Day 351
14:1	Day 194
14:13	Day 365
14:27	Day 24
15:1	Day 115
15:5	Day 246
15:13	Day 141

16:13	Day 111
16:13–15	Day 143
16:22	Day 196
16:24	Day 160
16:33	Day 11
17:23	Day 139

Acts

1:8	Day 195
2:41–42	Day 131
4:20	Day 38
5:29	Day 44
7:58–60	Day 296
12:5	Day 123

Romans

1:20	Day 221
5:3–5	Day 205
5:5	Day 8
6:23	Day 6
8:6	Day 260
8:26–27	Day 37
8:28	Days 39, 136
8:31	Day 62
8:31–32	Day 35
8:38–39	Day 78
11:33–36	Day 289
12:2	Day 132
12:6–8	Day 237
12:12	Days 60, 205
15:13	Days 28

1 Corinthians

6:19–20	Day 157
13:12	Day 41
13:13	Day 303
15:33	Day 216

2 Corinthians

1:3–4	Day 81
1:5	Day 243
1:8–9	Day 276
1:21–22	Day 202
4:16	Day 134
4:16–17	Day 185
4:17	Day 34
4:18	Day 226
5:7	Day 54
9:6–8	Day 161
10:5	Days 122, 209
10:17	Day 133
12:9	Day 108
12:9–10	Day 311

Galatians

1:10	Day 309
5:13–14	Day 129
5:22–23	Days 155, 188
6:9–10	Day 333

Ephesians

2:10	Day 293
3:16–19	Day 164
3:17–19	Day 97
3:20	Days 45, 224
4:2	Day 227
4:2–3	Day 178
5:15–16	Day 241
5:19–20	Day 315
6:10	Days 14, 287

6:12–17 .... Day 231
6:18 .... Day 107
6:18–19 .... Day 177

Philippians
1:9 .... Day 147
2:4 .... Day 198
2:14 .... Day 305
3:13–14 .... Day 242
4:4 .... Days 206, 297
4:6 .... Days 10, 93
4:7 .... Day 82
4:11–13 .... Day 239
4:13 .... Day 26
4:19 .... Day 90

Colossians
1:3 .... Day 317
2:6–7 .... Days 171, 288
3:2 .... Day 255
3:8 .... Day 337
3:12 .... Day 32
3:15 .... Day 156
3:23 .... Day 244
4:2 .... Days 13, 72

1 Thessalonians
1:2 .... Day 167
5:17 .... Days 2, 162
5:18 .... Days 46, 49
5:21–22 .... Day 251

1 Timothy
2:1 .... Day 53
2:2–3 .... Day 267
2:3–6 .... Day 17

4:12 .... Day 145
5:8 .... Day 126

2 Timothy
1:5 .... Day 352
1:7 .... Day 9

Hebrews
4:12 .... Day 29
4:14–16 .... Day 33
4:16 .... Day 254
6:19 .... Day 248
7:25 .... Day 184
10:25 .... Day 51
12:2 .... Day 146
12:5–6 .... Day 329
12:7–9 .... Day 330
13:5 .... Day 285
13:6 .... Day 12
13:7 .... Day 349
13:8 .... Days 212, 261
13:15 .... Day 112

James
1:2–3 .... Day 104
1:5–7 .... Day 73
1:19 .... Day 137
1:22–25 .... Day 169
1:27 .... Day 213
3:8 .... Day 117
4:7–8 .... Day 278
4:8 .... Day 55
5:13 .... Day 301

1 Peter
1:7–9 .... Day 297

1:8–9	Day 176
2:9	Day 240
3:4	Day 106
3:15–16	Day 103
4:8	Day 323
4:12	Day 149
5:7	Days 158, 197
5:8–9	Day 151

2 Peter
1:5–8	Day 335

1 John
1:5	Day 269
1:5–7	Day 359
1:8–9	Day 113
2:3–6	Day 165
4:10	Day 4
5:13–15	Day 23

3 John
1:2	Day 109

Jude
1:20–21	Day 299

Revelation
21:4	Day 153
22:13	Day 284

Check Out This Fun Faith Map!

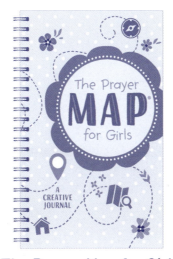

The Prayer Map for Girls
978-1-68322-559-1

This prayer journal is a fun and creative way to fully experience the power of prayer. Each page guides you to write out thoughts, ideas, and lists. . .creating a specific "map" for you to follow as you talk to God. Each map includes a spot to record the date, so you can look back on your prayers and see how God has worked in your life.

Spiral Bound

Find This and More from Barbour Publishing at Your Favorite Bookstore or www.barbourbooks.com